SPACES FOR SILENCE

Originally published in 1964 by Franciscan Herald Press.
Republished in 2022 by Joannes Press with the permission of the Poor Clares
of the Monastery of Our Lady of Guadalupe, Roswell, New Mexico.

ISBN: 978-1-7371230-2-6

Cover image:
Frederic Edwin Church, *The Monastery of San Pedro (Our Lady of the Snows)*
(1879)

No part of this book may be reproduced, stored in a retrieval system, or transmitted in any form, or by any means, electronic, mechanical, or otherwise, without the prior written permission of the publisher, except by a reviewer, who may quote brief passages in a review.

All parenthetical Scripture citations are editorial editions by Joannes Press. The numbering used comes from the *Douay-Rheims* translation of the Holy Bible.

www.joannespress.com

SPACES FOR SILENCE

MOTHER MARY FRANCIS, P.C.C.

Acknowledgments

These essays first appeared in the following magazines, and are reprinted with the kind permission of the editors: REVIEW FOR RELIGIOUS, *The Silence and the Song;* THE CORD, *The Heart of Her Giving, Up Until This Time, Clare: Woman of Faith, St. Clare: Saint for Now;* TODAY, *The Art of Praise, Spaces for Silence, The Sacredness of Things, The Single Tragedy, Freedom From Surfeit;* AVE MARIA, *Christmas in the Cloister;* SPIRIT, *Poetry and the Contemplative;* FRIAR, *Drums of Chatter, Simplicity, Chesterton and the Franciscan Heart.*

Contents

Preface, by Mother Mary Angela, P.C.C.
i

Preface, by Sister Maura, S.S.N.D
ii

I. Spaces for Silence
1

II. The Drums of Chatter
7

III. Christmas in the Cloister
12

IV. The Heart of Her Giving
24

V. Freedom from Surfeit
34

VI. Poetry and the Contemplative
41

VII. The Sacredness of Things
51

VIII. The Art of Praise
57

IX. Creative Spiritual Leadership
65

X. The Silence and the Song
79

XI. Chesterton and the Franciscan Heart
88

XII. Simplicity
95

XIII. The Single Tragedy
102

XIV. Clare of Assisi: Saint for Now
108

XV. Clare of Assisi: Woman of Faith
117

XVI. Up Until This Time We Have Done Nothiing
123

About the Author
130

Preface

"We live together in the silences of His Love. Let us abide there."
—Mother Abbess

So reads the inscription on the flyleaf of the newly-published *Spaces for Silence*, written in the firm, flowing hand of Mother Mary Francis, P.C.C. in 1964, the very year in which she had been elected to the service of abbess of the Roswell Poor Clare community. Hardly could she have imagined what lay ahead in the forty-one years of her abbatial service, during which she would guide her community into a new millennium.

At that time, the Second Vatican Council was nearing its conclusion; it would fall to Mother Mary Francis, then in her forties, to guide her community—and before long, the federation to which her community belonged—through the storms and tempests generated by widespread misinterpretation of the Church's teaching on religious life. Like her handwriting, her vision of the true summons to renewal and ressourcement flowing from the Council documents was clear and firm and unwavering; it would guide those who listened through the uncharted waters of those tumultuous times.

Could Mother Mary Francis have foreseen just how timely her reflections on silence would be in the years to come, when the technological revolution would make available personal and portable drums of chatter for all who could hold a cell phone? Mother Francis walks as a true "apostle of silence" into our media-muddled minds, to teach us once again the necessity to establish spaces for silence in which we can learn to know ourselves and the God Who loves us.

Mother wrote of freedom from surfeit in the time before luxury was confused with necessity. She reflects insightfully and incisively on simplicity with us who have more than a "fairly good start down the winding paths of complexity." She ponders the sacredness of things for the benefit of an age in which reverence for the rights of God and man are in perilous danger. All of her reflections, though written in quite different times, have urgent and opportune messages for our own troubled and troubling days.

If I may be permitted a final observation about Mother's handwriting: it was always legible and beautiful. Her poet's heart, sensitive to beauty wherever God set it in her path, was possessed of an urgency to share that beauty with others through her songs of love. She wrote prose of great clarity and poetry of exquisite beauty, with but one goal: to lead our hearts to repose in the singing silence of the One Who is Himself Truth and Goodness and Beauty.

Mother Mary Angela, P.C.C.,
Abbess of the Poor Clare Monastery of
Our Lady of Guadalupe, Roswell, New Mexico
July 26, 2022, the 78th anniversary of the religious
profession of Mother Mary Francis, P.C.C.

Preface to the 1964 Edition

Tell the good news.

Tell the glad tidings of redemption.

When God became man, angels and men were missioned to tell the good news. From Christmas night when flights of angels announced peace on earth to men of good will to Easter morning when Christ bade Mary Magdalen go and tell the brethren the glad tidings, love found ways to make Love known.

Mother Mary Francis, P.C.C., Abbess of the Poor Clare Monastery of Our Lady of Guadalupe in Roswell, New Mexico—living in one of the most penitential and joyous of the religious orders of the Church—retells the glad tidings in a collection of essays called *Spaces For Silence*.

Her way of telling is as intimate and conversational as the talk that lingers through the hours of a happy family reunion. She writes in this way because she is a woman in love. She loves with her total being, and—because God has given her a reverence for words—she uses words to set free the totality of her love that it may reach all the children of God, each as an individual.

What does she write about? Silence, of course. Only through silence will man come to contemplation. Only in contemplation will he find the One for Whom he longs.

She writes of human things: the story of a first Christmas in the new and primitively poor monastery in Roswell; the delight of freedom; the art of praise; the sacredness of things; poetry and contemplation. There are essays about lovers: Francis, Clare, Thomas Aquinas, Our Lady of the Visitation, Christ our Life.

Mother Mary Francis has an extraordinarily honest view of reality, a reality illuminated by faith, irradiated with joy.

She understands that the world for which the Poor Clares pray through the night and day is one in which international and national stresses, cold wars, burning hates, false ideologies, poverty, speed, automation and gross advertising fragmentize the order and peace that man was made for.

She does not sentimentalize monastic life either. The unfinished enclosure fence "ends like a hiccough"; the nose is red, the feet are blue with cold. She is a realist because she knows that God is the only Reality, and she looks at warts and broken water pipes with the sure awareness that God Incarnate looked at the reality of His world with absolute honesty.

To accept reality in this way one must see it illuminated by faith. Mother Mary Francis writes as a person who believes what God has said because He said it. He said: "I am the Way" (Jn 14:6). She tells about following Him. He said: "If anyone wishes to come after Me, let him deny himself, take up his cross, and follow Me" (Mt 16:24). She tells about discipline and penance accepted with

Preface

gladness because Christ chose suffering as an expression of love. He said: "Do not be afraid, little flock..." (Lk 12:32). She tells of trust and unwavering confidence in the providence of God. He said: "These things I have spoken to you that My joy may be in you" (Jn 15:11)...She tells us the secret of joy.

This joy that Christ promised to those who live and love in His way enriches the essays. It is a joy to be shared, to be given away.

Come, taste the joy of the glory that is yours. Alleluja!
Show your gratitude to God. Alleluja!
For He has invited you to enter into the kingdom of heaven. Alleluja!
(Entrance Chant: Whit Tuesday)

There is another dynamic movement in these essays. It is a creative spirit. St. Paul said: "We are God's co-workers" (1 Cor 3:9). Human action is upheld and given its own life by the divine action in man.

Unwittingly, Mother Mary Francis gives us intimations of creative action in herself and her Sisters. God gave to each a deposit of talent. It is used for His glory. In the monastic community, the Sisters seed and spade vegetable and flower gardens; work in printing and crafts; sing, chant, and play musical instruments; study and read; scrub, bake, mend; pray and live penitentially—do all things with whatever skills they may command because their action is grafted on the action of God in their lives.

As one reads, a curious thing happens: the reader, too, becomes a creator. Creativity, like goodness, like love, overflows.

In *Spaces For Silence*, Mother Mary Francis communicates the spirit of silence, that great resource of the human spirit. She shows silence working within, making a depth in which love may grow strong; silence teaching mind and heart to pray; silence preparing the soul for joy.

Spaces for Silence

Before the reader has finished an essay, he will know that he has been welcomed into the singing silence of Franciscan love. He will read and reread the essays, discovering as he reads, the place for silence in his own heart. In that silence he may listen to God.

This is a book that tells of glad tidings.

Sister Maura, S.S.N.D.
Feast of Our Lady's Nativity
September 8, 1964

I

SPACES FOR SILENCE

TO LIVE CLOSELY with a stranger all of one's life might seem more a contradiction in terms than a formidable prospect. Does not continual companionship eliminate the possibility of a stranger-relationship? We might think so, except for the reality of so many of us living just that way. And who is the elusive stranger we find unfathomable simply because we have never tried to fathom him—the one really not so much unfathomable as merely unfathomed? It is the stranger we see in the mirror. The girl with the bouffant coiffure, the boy in the bright yellow socks.

It is a strange paradox that we who have inherited from our first parents, those frightened and fig-aproned figures in a ruined paradise, an interest in the ego so absorbing as to unbalance our entire perspective, should, by the same legacy, own an astonishing stubbornness of refusal to look at ourselves. Each of us has his private amphitheatre where he battles the fascinating temptation to pretend the entire universe revolves about himself. There may be no cheering fans in the grandstands, but some of the most brilliant battles in history have been fought in just such lonely arenas of the spirit. However, some of us may never even enter the arena, never see any reason for battle, because we have never really got around to seeing ourselves. We can be so occupied in looking at our external selves that we have no time left for seeing our interior selves. Perhaps again we do not even know *how* to look, how to get the interior mirror into focus so that we do not see ourselves after the manner of those cunningly curved mirrors which show us now all forehead, now all chin, here like an overdone El Greco, there like a super-fattened Raphael. For, quiet is the focus, and silence is the mirror.

Silence is a great art, and one increasingly difficult to perfect with just about every detail of living conspiring against it. We cannot hear birdsong for automobile horns. Scenery has retreated behind the billboards. And you can have your thinking done for you by the loudest slogans and the glossiest magazines—served up for you as neatly and painlessly as a TV dinner on its aluminum plate. None of which is to register any particular complaint against a horn, a billboard, a slogan, or a magazine; but only to observe that our lives work more and more against silence and thus against the rich experiences of the interior life. Yet, without silence we shall go on living like a stranger in our own inner court. This remains true, however much the world in general may prefer to conceive of silence as monkish and medieval, a quaint old art like brass-rubbing or sampler-stitching.

Even our attitude toward monastic silence is likely to be more tolerant and respectful than interested. The silent Trappists inspire a delicate shudder; the Poor Clares' one hour of talk per day seems real starvation rations—until we come up with the happy afterthought that monks and nuns would not have anything to talk about in any case.

It is true that the things which promise to be most penitential in the beginning are not much so at all. Silence is one of these. What is a sharp discipline at the outset becomes progressively a response, a refuge, a school, and then a home. If twenty nuns bring the riches of long silence to one hour of talk, the result will understandably be that unself-conscious gaiety and spontaneous warm interchange which mark the recreation hour in a cloister. But silence is not just a device for nuns. It is the first of the liberal arts and the coloring of the humanities.

It is always painful to be long in the company of the person who simply never stops talking. Yet, to spend our lives chattering away at ourselves is a much craftier attack on our own spirit. We know that our best friends are those with whom we can spend the longest spaces in silence. It is the occasional friend with whom we feel we must keep the patter going. Sometimes we treat our very self as merely the occasional friend.

Now, the giant "I" is a liar from the beginning. Witness the sorrowing psalmist who yet has a trace of a smile on his sigh: "Every man is a liar" (Ps 115:11). And no man more than the man one is! We are all so utterly devoted to ourselves. And, basically, that is God's plan. Our Lord was a very plainspoken man. Even His most subtle parables were lifted from commonplace details and circumstances. And He cautioned us to love others as we love ourselves, thus making it clear that love for oneself is not only justifiable and good, but the very touchstone of charity. True, on one far day He was to ask us to soar beyond this plane and love as He had loved, but the self was Christ's starting point in the three-year course He gave on perfection.

Unfortunately, the pure and beautiful love for one's self suffered a strange disorder on that fatal day when an apple became the only desirable fruit on the market for the only man and woman in the world. The kind of self-love we inherited is a low enough thing, hinging on a sense of one's importance which is expressed in one's infallible opinions, one's inspired plans, one's elect temperament. Strange disorder indeed! For, the fundamental awareness of one's own importance is sound and true. We are so important as to have been loved with an everlasting love and bought at a great price.

Some really logical conclusions from a *right* understanding of our importance could run like this: that opinions of others do not really matter at all to one who is cherished by an omniscient God; that plans are nursery toys to one who is adult in clinging to a changeless Will; that one's own makeup is a matter of potter's clay for a tender if terrible Hand. To reason like this is to be released from the compelling herd, to enter into that joy which consists in waiting on God's plans, and to put aside care about "the development of one's personality" in favor of letting Christ develop the personality He has created. For such reasoning, silence is the great indispensable. This concept of one's actual worth simply cannot be formed outside silence, particularly not by having many people talk at us about many things.

Even music needs its pauses, and often enough the pause indicates the composer's consummate art. That we are pathetically in need of more pauses in our life's personal score could scarcely be better demonstrated than in the ads for fall-out shelters complete with TV. The unexpressed idea seems to be that if one is huddling against fall-out death, balancing on the very rim of eternity, one must have some way to fill in the time. This is a modern version of the old story about the man in the lighthouse who was so accustomed to a signal shot being fired each midnight that on the night the shot failed to be fired, he sat up in bed yelling, "What was that?"

It is possible to establish spaces for silence in any life. Our Lady of Wisdom ever "kept all these things, conferring with herself in her heart" (Lk 2:19). We learn such marvelous things about God, about others, but most of all about ourselves in silence. Everything around us is conspiring to make us "self-conscious" on a shampoo and dentifrice level. And the triumph of this noisy outer invasion is to make us overlook our head in favor of our hair, our vision in favor of our eyelashes, our destiny in favor of our dress. It takes much sitting beside the lakes of silence to become "self-conscious" to that point where the stunning realities of the truths we mouthed as children break in upon us. Such realities as that we are each a unique masterpiece of God's creative love, each with a peculiar destiny to fulfill and a particular glory to attain. That we are created to know God, to love Him, wait on Him, and rejoice with Him now on earth and forever in heaven.

When we sink down into silence and try to take these things in, problems become surprisingly simplified and life gloriously enriched. After all, it is quite possible to love God in a fall-out shelter. And if He is present in our soul by grace, we can assuredly rejoice in or out of any shelter. There will be wonderful riches to enjoy there, joys to savor there, security there. Silence will have taught us who we are and Who God is. And we won't need TV in our fall-out shelter with such sufficiencies as these.

The world is always crying for new apostles. Apostles of progress, dedicated men and women. Maybe what we most need is some apostles of silence, some young men and women dedicated to reality, self-conscious in the startling sense of being conscious of the God-like dignity of their selves. All the mirrors will not tell us how really beautiful we potentially are. Silence will show us. All the noise and the hurry and the clamorous camouflages of life cover us with a cloud of dust who were meant to be covered with a cloud of glory.

"When all things were in quiet silence, and the night was in the midst of its course, Your Almighty Word, O God, leaped down from heaven" (Wis 18:14-15). That is the way the Almighty Word will leap down into hearts, too. What a tremendous mission that would be—to restore some spaces for silence in a world overpopulated with noise!

It takes heroic self-discipline to master the art of silence, enormous strength of purpose to accept the revelations of self discovered in silence. But once a clearing is made, when we have incinerated our interior rubble and knelt down in the space of silence within us to make the acquaintance of ourselves, God's grace comes sweeping into the clearing. And even as we learn to know ourselves, we learn to know Him. This is, in a sense, to know everything. And it is to know so much more enduringly than the people stacking up facts in the noisy warehouses of non-essentials.

Apostle of silence witnessing to "the kingdom of God which is within you" (Lk 17:21)! Missionary to the deepest homeland of one's own spirit! Anyone?

11

THE DRUMS OF CHATTER

NOT LONG BEFORE his death, Coventry Patmore expressed the wistful hope that posterity would respect his writing. "For," he said, "I have always respected posterity. I have never written anything when I had nothing to say." It should not be too difficult for many of us to swell the chorus of that quiet boast—since many of us do not write! The honest declaration that we have never spoken when we had nothing to say might be more remote.

"Nerves" have become very fashionable in our generation. As Father Gillis observed, people now speak of "my psychiatrist" as casually as their grandparents spoke of "my dentist" or "my tailor." We blame a great deal of this taut-nerved tension on our environment. Speed, noise, clangor everywhere. But perhaps more noise emanates *from* us than assaults us! Perhaps we are talking our energy and even our essence away when three-quarters of the time we have all of nothing to say.

Conversation is a great art. It enriches our personality, enlarges our mental horizons and matures our opinions. Conversely, chatter depletes our forces, narrows our vision and kills thoughtful opinions aborning. Conversation is the fruit of silence and reflection. Talk is the firstborn child of noise. That explains why those who know how and when to be silent have so much to say when they speak, and why strangers to silence have so little.

Maybe the proof of our underevaluation of personal quiet is the fact that so many persons are startled and then amused that silent, contemplative nuns should have a lively interest in conversation at all. What would cloistered nuns possibly have to talk about, even if they could talk? They live with the same small group of women continuously. The scenery never changes. Most of them do not know their own telephone number. The single hour of recreation must be a grim affair of exchanging reminders that we must all one day die, and possibly commenting brightly on the crack in the enclosure wall.

Just to increase the handicap, talk of food, illnesses (you can't subject anyone to a full account of your operation!), worldly amusements, dreams, private penances and a few other topics are all ruled out of the list of proper conversational subjects. Once a puzzled priest inquired as to what we talk about after the first couple of years in the cloister have exhausted each nun's private stock of amusing and enlivening anecdotes brought in with her from the world. "I guess you must have to tell lies," he concluded sadly. Yet we go on, year after year, never accomplishing the linguistic feat of sharing all the riches of a silent day with our Sisters in the hour of conversation that marks each day's close. No one has time to invent any entertaining lies! We find the truth of being alive and together not only so much stranger but also so much more wonderful than fiction. If we chattered all day long, however, we might really be driven to fabrications by evening.

What does the prodigious chatterer give us to take into the fabric of our own lives? Nothing. What does the incessant talker really contribute to conversation? Nothing. We are wearied by the constant drums of chatter, and most wearied when we beat the drums ourselves.

St. Luke is fond of telling us how our Lady "kept all these things, pondering them in her heart" (Lk 2:19). She had many things to keep and to ponder: the secrets of God and the mysteries of His Love. Those secrets and mysteries were laid in the silent repository of her soul. They were not run through a sieve of idle talk. The Latin expresses it more precisely and appealingly when it says, *"conferens in corde suo."* Our Lady "conferred" with her soul about all these things.

Out of these silent conferences came a sublime poem, *"Magnificat anima mea Dominum,"* a short sentence at a wedding banquet, and a question in the temple at Jerusalem. So, all true Christian poets ever since then have warmed their songs at our Lady's flame. All generations thank her for the miracle of divine courtesy she won at Cana. And theologians continue to ponder and propound her gentle mother's reproof to the Son of God in the temple.

Precisely because our Lady had so much to tell us, she said very little.

We have all experienced in some measure or other how silence is a party to the most important things in life, whereas idle talk belongs to the trivia of life. With the new acquaintance, we feel obliged to talk a great deal because there is not yet the communion of spirit which brings silent enjoyment. We batter the ears of strangers with comments on the weather, TV ratings, sardines in mustard, or the latest soap chips slogan. With our oldest friends, we can be silent for long intervals. And out of those rich silences comes the exchange of ideas and the words we shall remember.

So it is in cloisters. Because we cannot express each new thought that enters our minds at the very moment of its entrance, but must put it aside for the one evening hour of conversation, we become expert at separating the chaff from the wheat. So little that we might have said without pondering, without first "conferring" with ourselves, is worth the saying, after all. That explains the vitality of the recreation hour in cloisters. What each nun has to say is the product of her silence, and so it is worth the listening even when it is only light-hearted banter. Light banter, too, can be an art!

The great Dom Marmion was said to have been the very mainspring of recreation conversation at his abbey.[1] No one was a more delightful talker, no one gayer, no one wittier. Yet, when this holy religious once received a tremendous grace from God, he who was "the life" of the recreation hours said very simply that he thought it might be God's reward for the fact that he had not failed against monastic silence for the past several years.

Conversation is coming to be something of a lost art in our age. It is our business to reclaim it. Relatively few are called to live in the silence of the cloister, but each of us has a cloister in his or her own heart. If we do not learn how to dwell there happily, to take our mental rest and some of our mental nourishment there, we are untrue to ourselves. Each of us has a great deal to give to

---

[1] Blessed Dom Columba Marmion, O.S.B., was an Irish born priest who became a Benedictine monk and later the Abbot of the Maredsous Abbey in Belgium. He was a great spiritual writer penning such classics as *Christ, the Life of the Soul* and *Christ, the Ideal of the Monk*

others. We discover what it is in silence and we dispense it in conversation.

The spiritually impoverished person is the one whose heart-cloister is always untenanted. A whole personality is warped by noise while dust gathers in that interior cloister. But the man or woman who has learned to think independently in that cloistered silence, to "confer" with himself before conferring with the whole world at large, is the one whose words will be worth remembering. His friends will learn to respect him and to gather strength from his words because, like Coventry Patmore, he had something to say when he spoke.

He will be the one to help restore the art of conversation to its proper place of dignity and honor. Maybe he will join the conversation-piece of Chesterton, Belloc and Baring, and grow to the race of mental giants who first learned how to confer with themselves in the cloister of the heart and then had so much to say when they spoke.

There has never been a great conversationalist who was not skilled in the art of listening. And the art of listening is perfected only in silence and reflection. Our Lady was the most perfect listener who ever lived. That is why her few words are the most memorable ever uttered by a creature. We think in silence. Inspiration, like grace, is given to quiet; for, its delicate voice is drowned in noise. Our Lady of Wisdom can teach us the art of listening if we ask her. She will share her gift of quiet with us if we desire it.

> Mary was full of listening
> And the Word
> Was uttered in her silence
> Like a bellstroke.

III

Christmas in the Cloister

N O, IT SCARCELY EVER snows in New Mexico, at least, not in Roswell, the natives told us. Oh, well, we thought, we don't need snow. It was only that the spreading acre at the east of the enclosure looked so dreary. We had been in our new monastery for a month and a half, and now it was the day before Christmas Eve. Maybe that was why the big field looked so drably brown. We felt everything should be beautiful with life these last blessed days before the anniversary of the coming of Life and Beauty.

"We'll plant trees in the spring," Mother Abbess soothed us. "And we'll move some of those magnificent japonicas around the house over to the edge of the field." She grew more enthusiastic as the gardener's heart of her expanded under these first mental brush-strokes on the east grounds in the springtime. There would be flower beds all along the driveway, and we would steal half the Extern Sisters' pampas grass and plant it in the cloister, and we would have rows of green peas in the field and sweet-smelling cantaloupes, and, and, and. We felt comforted. But today we would not look at the sere brown field except to remember that Bethlehem had been bare, too.

Sister Sacristan rang the rising bell five minutes earlier on the morning of Christmas Eve because the solemn Christmas Martyrology would be sung at Prime. I sprang off our straw sack with the reflex action which is the happy reward of several years of determined effort, and made a sleepy sign of the cross. I knelt down and kissed the floor of our cell, as it is our custom. It tasted cold and smelled fragrantly of the vigorous waxing to which I had subjected it the day before. "Oh, my God, I offer you this, my first act of obedience and mortification…" I began. My eyes were entirely open now, and I blinked dazedly. Had God accepted this first morning offering with a miracle, I wondered? Our cell was so bright!

The fifteen watt bulb in the dormitory hall furnished the only light for all our cells, and what illumination this Poor Clare chandelier managed to provide through cell doors open two or three inches to admit it was rather less than dazzling. The light that was washing down our habit skirt this morning and gleaming on my bare feet was something different. Then I saw it—the snow! Snow singing, laughing, whirling everywhere! Snow insistent on the window ledge, snow fitting great ballerina skirts on the elm trees. It tore the last cobwebs of sleep from my eyes before the cold water in the pitcher followed to shiver me awake. I brushed my teeth in record time and swept down the dormitory stairs with a vigor I usually reserve for post-breakfast-coffee-time, and slid across the community room floor to the east window.

There was the big field. But, no, it was a huge lake of light! Thick masses of stars reached down arms of light toward our new little monastery. The white grounds reached back. Evidently our Lord had decided to tear up the weather forecasts and behindcasts for Roswell this year of our first coming. I looked at the light streaming up from the snow and down from the sky again; and I walked slowly into the choir, a little shaken with the beauty of the embrace. We could not afford to decorate. The Lord had.

Some of the nuns were already in their stalls. I genuflected before our tiny altar where the brave paper flowers no longer smiled on this solemn Vigil. I bowed to the assembled nuns and wondered why the cold choir seemed so warm this morning. Then I discovered it! Under the candle shelf which was always referred to with dignity as "the cloister altar" was a piece of log. So this was why Mother Vicaress had been sawing that log last week and hollowing it out with the care of a Michelangelo fingering his stone! There were a few sprigs of evergreen in the hollow. It rested on them. The Crib.

Mother Abbess had said it just could not be managed. We could not afford a Crib set. And if Mother Vicaress did fashion one out of branches like the one she had so painstakingly made for the extern chapel, there would simply be no place to put it. We could barely squeeze ourselves into the midget-sized choir. We could rejoice that there was a Crib in the public chapel, and we could remember the big Crib in our former monastery with the lights blooming around it and the tall trees on guard behind it, couldn't we? We could. We were pioneers now. We knew that, didn't we? We did. It was only that our knowledge was a trifle grim, and our rejoicing by memory in what we could not see was a bit restrained. Our pioneering had never weighed on us thus far any more heavily than laughter. But no Crib. . . this was sheer nuns' tragedy, and it had unmanned us all. Now, on the morning of Christmas Eve, we were delivered! Mother Abbess had found a way after all, as she has a most marvelous gift for finding a way. There was the Crib.

It was made of marble-dust and stood all of five inches high. Our Blessed Mother's mantle was faintly pink in the candlelight, and the brown of St. Joseph's cloak looked appropriately long-worn. Between them, the tiniest possible figurine of the Holy Child waved liliputian fists for the joy of being born under the altar in the Roswell cloister. The Crib was, past any possibility of comparison, the most beautiful Crib in the world.

The Psalms of Prime swept around the small choir, seeming to push back its wall with their glory until it was suddenly spacious. *Crastina die! Crastina die!* Tomorrow, tomorrow, tomorrow! the Office kept singing; and I wondered whether Holy Church was really going to be able to contain the thunder of her exultation until tomorrow.

It is only today, and not tomorrow, my heart whispered to the elfin Christ in the marble dust Crib. You should not be here! It had always been our custom to arrange the big stable in the choir the day before, but the Crib with its drift of white blanket and small, scented pillow was left empty until Christmas Matins when Mother Abbess placed the carved bambino from Jerusalem in his ancient place. But even Reverend Mother could conceive of no plan for removing this one-inch marble-dust Jesus from His five-inch Crib. So, there He lay, ahead of schedule, watching Sister Juliana from small grave eyes as she went to the lectern in the middle of the choir to sing the Christmas Martyrology, the solemn announcement of His Birth.

Our month-old community had no novices, so Sister Margaret and I supplied as candlebearers. It was enough to fit singer and lectern into the middle of our choir. Candlebearers beside her were out of the question. So we stood in front of her, so close to the hollowed log with its five-inch Crib that our candle flames made two small rings of radiance about it.

Sister Juliana's voice was marking off the centuries as lightly as minutes: "In the year, from the creation of the world, when in the beginning God created heaven and earth, five thousand one hundred and ninety-nine; from the flood, two thousand nine hundred and fifty-seven; from the birth of Abraham, two thousand and fifteen…" Then the singing tempo slowed, and I knew why her voice trembled just a little. She had too great a message for the voice of one small nun to bear: "Jesus Christ, having been conceived of the Holy Ghost, and nine months having elapsed since His Conception, is born in Bethlehem of Juda, having become Man of the Virgin Mary."

We fell on our knees. The singing halted. I thought our breathing did, too. "God so loved the world as to give His only-begotten Son…" (Jn 3:16). The mystery of joy which is Christmas reached down into our souls until it found their marrow.

I looked at the marble-dust Crib and at the axe-cuts in the log where Mother Vicaress had missed her mark a little. And I whispered my own addition to the Christmas Martyrology: "And nineteen hundred and fifty years after the Birth of the Son of God in Bethlehem, is born a new cloister in an old farmhouse in the southwest United States where He shall henceforth be loved and praised through generation and generation. Amen."

When Mother Abbess turned off the choir lights after Prime, we sat back on our heels, Franciscan fashion, to make our meditation. It was not difficult. The splendors of moon and stars still shining on snow, filled the choir. The little marble-dust Crib glowed in the dark. It seemed to grow bigger and bigger and to occupy the whole choir.

Christmas in the Cloister

There were only eight of us in the cloister, and space was very limited in our new monastery. But we covered mile upon mile! It was Christmas Eve; and even if they have been in a monastery only one month, nuns could not conceive of a Christmas not preceded by a fever of housecleaning. The scope for our talents was somewhat limited that year, but we scrubbed and polished and scoured all available accouterments of monastic living. And Sister Catherine, suddenly borne down upon by a last-minute inspiration, pulled the kitchen stove apart and began boiling the burners in some mysterious solution whose formula is known only to herself and her Creator. Less talented and a little lacking in confidence, I surveyed the skeleton of our stove, our greatest material possession, and sent up a vague prayer to our Lady that Sister Catherine would get the thing back together for Christmas dinner.

Outside, the Extern Sisters were swaying on ladders, decorating their little altar with all the skill of the San Pietrini in Rome. Then suddenly, very suddenly, it was time for the first Vespers of Christmas, the opening of the solemn Office of the Nativity of the Son of God. And it was the moment to which all moments of our past six weeks in Roswell had led. For, at last, we had a bell. A tower bell! A big, handsome bell given us by the Trappist monks. And the tower bell was going to peal its first remarks for Christmas Vespers.

Of course, we had no tower; but that was a minor matter as long as we had a tower *bell*. Long conferences held by Mother Abbess, Mother Vicaress, and the Novice Mistress had produced a major feat of nuns' engineering. Two heavy metal pipes, bought from a junk dealer at a most marvelous bargain, had been set upright in two deep holes in the ground outside the porch door. Suspended between them was our bell, San Miguel, making lavish pretense that he was in a tower.

Spaces for Silence

There was, to be sure, no question of pulling the bell-rope *down* unless you stood in some sort of subterranean chamber which we had no time to dig on Christmas Eve. So San Miguel's rope moved on a horizontal instead of a vertical plane. The big bell fell in with Poor Clare ingenuity with a right good will. When Mother Abbess herself rang it for the first time, San Miguel sang from his iron heart to proclaim the coming of the King. He said various other things, too, to the listening countryside: that there was now a cloister in Roswell and that it had, if not a tower, at least a tower bell. He talked of pioneering and of peace and of Redemption.

Mother came inside looking very much like an abbess who had a tower bell. Her nose was red and her toes were blue, and there were snowflakes set in a small crown on her veil and trimming her shawl with ermine. But she had other things to think about now. She solemnly intoned the First Vespers of Christmas, and when we all chanted together: "Tomorrow the iniquity of the world shall be blotted out, and the Savior of the world shall reign over us," we knew it was true.

We thought we did not need a Christmas tree. We had our marble-dust Crib and our tower bell and our snow.

These were accidentals enough for what we carried in our hearts, an imponderable and unpriced burden of joy. But when the Extern Sisters begged a little tree, and when Father Ambrose, O.F.M., pushed the doorbell with his elbow because his hands were full of lights and ornaments for us, we discovered that, suddenly, we needed a tree very much!

There is always this paradox about the accidental joys of life: only those who do not really need them can really appreciate their worth. Only those who have given them up know how to savor them. When you surrender to God all the small pleasures which once seemed important, you get an amazing return. Beyond the spaciousness of soul you feel in knowing that you have nothing but the essential, which is love, is something else. It is the stunning realization that, having relinquished all pleasures because of their relative unimportance, you have suddenly understood their real importance! St. Teresa is reputed to have once remarked that "penance is penance, and pheasant is pheasant." What is sure is that a person who has never tried penance cannot really appreciate pheasant.

God has studded life with a thousand small pleasurable surprises, but when we grasp and snatch at them, we do not really see them at all. Or, we can gulp them down so fast that they bring us nothing but spiritual indigestion and, finally, that state which to a Poor Clare is the least understandable of all states: boredom. It is easy to forget how to be surprised. And taking all good things for granted is the most perilous degree of ingratitude. Worse than a virile or even vicious ingratitude, this supine thanklessness is too blasé to be militantly anything. I have known many Poor Clares, tall and short, quick-tempered and gentle, shy and vocal, domestic-minded and intellectual, musical and tone-deaf; but I have never run into a blasé Poor Clare. I have never met a bored one.

It was that way with the tree, our first Christmas. At home, all of us had taken the tree for granted. Each Christmas time, someone went out and bought the tree. You took down the boxes of ornaments from the top shelves, sneezing at the dust on the boxes. And you decorated the tree. Everyone had a tree. But now we were pioneers on a new foundation. We could not put down one of our scarce dollars for a tree. We had no ornaments, nor even any top shelves for storing them. And we knew it did not matter at all. That is probably why we quite lost our heads over *this* Christmas tree! When we are convinced that we have no right to life's ornamentals, they assume their rightful proportions if they are sometimes loaned to us.

Spaces for Silence

We hoisted the little tree up onto the community room table, and it is safe to say that no skinny evergreen balding at the top and beaten at the bottom had ever before been so admired. Christmas Eve is a day of complete silence in the monastery, when even the usual recreation hour is sacrificed. But, without a word, we talked to one another as we hung on our tree the decorations received from the friars. We talked with the love in our eyes for one another and for a small Savior Who was having a birthday. We talked with the quick movements of our chapped hands and cold bare feet. We talked our Poor Clare family language whose accents of silence can be mastered only in the cloister. And when at the end, we all stood back and sighed: "Ah!" together, everyone understood clearly that everyone else was asking: "Sister, would you ever have imagined anything so beautiful?" and everyone else was answering: "No, I never could have!" although not a sentence was shaped aloud. It is all part of the mystery of sacrifice which is not so much a shutting out of things as of making room for them.

At 10:30 that Christmas Eve, we rose to chant the first Christmas Matins in our new monastery. The tiny Crib was enormous with meaning. The candle-shelf altar was opulent with our two very best candles. And a Protestant friend had thought to bring two flaming poinsettias for these strange new praying-nuns who had just come to Roswell. He did not understand us very well, but he suspected it was a good idea to have people in town who prayed for him all the time.

Volts of anticipation flashed about the little choir as the ancient chants of Matins caught us up into their glory. How it is possible to cherish depths of calm in your soul and still love the shivers of excitement in your heart, I would not pretend to explain. I only know it is possible. When Sister Juliana left the choir at the end of Matins to ring our "tower bell," we all knew it was a moment to press in the heart. And we all did.

"A Child is born for us," San Miguel cried out in thunderous strokes. "A Son is given to us," the big bell sang and sang, until the night caught up the peals with a thousand echoes. Back from the enclosure wall which ended as abruptly as a hiccough on the north side because we hadn't money to finish it, came the bell-talk: "A Child is born for us!" Off the slanting roof of the little monastery, the peals came sliding back down to us. I walked to the organ at the back of the choir (a distance of about five steps!) and took a quick look at the sky. Its midnight black was torn up with starlight. A sudden wind was ruffling the snow in the field and making it fall *up* which seemed somehow strangely appropriate on this night.

I began to play a quaint little pastoral of hills and shepherd pipes. The candles on the public altar outside raised their small, happy fires just above the grate curtain. And somewhere at the back of the grounds, the cows of our neighbor were calling out to San Miguel to tell them more of the Child and the Son. I remembered the ancient folk carol: "Winds were blowing, cows were lowing, stars were glowing, glowing, glowing! Jesus, Jesus, rest yo' head, yo' has got a manger bed." He had, right there under our candle-shelf altar.

After Midnight Mass and Lauds, we stood for brief minutes around our Christmas tree, the lovely thing! Then we crowded ourselves into the tiny refectory and feasted on hot tea and three cookies apiece. It was royal, everyone knew that. Good that we were not permitted to talk. It would have spoiled it. Before we went back to the dormitory, we stepped out on the porch and stood together looking up at the stars. No one felt cold. No one spoke. We had our Lord and one another. There could not possibly be any remarks to make about so great a miracle of love.

The next morning, though, after the third Mass, it was different. It is in the richness of silence that we discover something to say. It is part of the mystery of the Christmas tree, so wonderful because we could do without it and because we have given up the right to it. There is recreation all day on Christmas. Holy Father St. Francis wanted singing and rejoicing and laughter everywhere, with extra rations for the birds and all creatures great and small. We like to be his obedient daughters. So our cat had some salmon juice. And our dog had some sweet potato of which he is very fond. And we sat under our marvel of a tree and sang the old carols and talked of the many things we suddenly remembered we had to say to one another, and then fell silent, all of us together. "I wonder if Christmas will ever be quite as happy as this first one," someone asked, "when the community grows, and we have a real chapel and choir, and are not quite so crowded and poor…Will it still be as beautiful?" Her voice trailed off.

Now it is Christmas again, years later. And we know the answer.

We have a real chapel and choir. But we are still poor and we are still crowded because more have come to fill the empty choir stalls and the new refectory. And the wonder and beauty are the same because it is the same Child Who comes and the same love that awaits Him.

I watch the postulants and novices skidding down the cloisters with important-looking bundles of evergreen and holly. There is great commotion in the novitiate vestibule over how many of the available branches Martha may need to trim the Sacred Heart altar because, after all, Sister Judith has the heavy responsibility of stretching the supply to take care of the window in the chapter room and a wreath for the Novice Mistress' cell door, besides the novitiate altar! I smile, and wonder what has become of the young sophisticates who clacked into the cloister on their needle heels since last Christmas. They have somehow disappeared into children of St. Francis.

Then I watch Mother Vicaress flicking her critical artist's eye over the new Crib she has made from another and bigger log. I observe how young the old Sisters look at Christmastime as they flash by in the community room. I see Sister Catherine frowning in her "feastday recipes" looseleaf notebook with the absorption of a Chaucerian scholar over a Bell manuscript. And I notice how lightly Mother Abbess skims along the halls, and how the smile never quite disappears around the curve of her mouth.

So we get ready again. But how, I hear you ask? We have no shopping to do, no money to spend. We have no worries about whether Uncle Horace will like those green socks or not. It may snow. It probably won't. We do not care. Someone may donate a very large tree or a scrubby little one. Either will be beautiful to us. Somebody may give us some fish for Christmas dinner, or perhaps some ice cream instead. Either will make a triumph of a feast. What matters is the small figure in the Crib and the One it represents. What matters is the tremendous force of love which makes cloisters continue to spring up in every land the warm and tender love of women who have got free of everything that glitters and found the thing that shines.

IV

The Heart of Her Giving

IT IS PLEASANT to think of the Mother of God as the type of all ivory-tower "contemplatives." If it robs us of a bosom of compassion, it at least liberates us from the responsibility of imitating an open-eyed and wide-hearted Mother. The Gospel, however, has a way of upsetting comfortable ideas, and pulling our mental chairs-at-the-heart-of-cozy-notions right out from under us. Thus we are jarred to read that the greatest of all contemplatives reacted to the most staggering message ever sent from Heaven to earth, not by sinking down into an abyss of reflection, but by a very practical act of charity.

Mary was utterly simple. If God wished, of a sudden, to suspend the laws of nature and descend unto her ever-virginal womb, she would obey. Mary had the faith that tumbles mountains. Once her consent at the Annunciation was expressed, she *knew* that Almighty God lived beneath her heart, though there was only faith to tell her so. And Mary was also intensely practical. The angel had said that the aged Elizabeth was with child. Then she, Mary, would bear to her frail cousin the strength of the Omnipotence within her. Mary's first recorded deed after her conception of the Son of God was to bear Him to others, to give Him away. She knew, with the wisdom of holiness, that it is the only way to hold Him. And in this she proved herself the prototype of the authentic contemplative who receives only to give, who receives by giving, and in whom the two finally merge into one perfection.

It has become almost a truism—however mentally unabsorbed—that had Christians the zeal of Communists, it would be a question of the kingdom of Christ realizing immense gains of souls in the world today, instead of the kingdom of atheistic Communism making those immense losses of souls which constitute its malign victory. The blue flag of Mary and her Divine Son could supplant the red flag of state-idolatry if more Catholics took the trouble to wave it instead of being content with owning it. What of us religious? A sterile ownership is a precarious security. For, we are all really stewards, we Franciscans, and stewards only. And it will be not only to the materially opulent, but likewise to the spiritually affluent, that Mary's Son will one day issue the disconcerting command: Give an account of your stewardship (Lk 16:2)! The inheritors of seraphic love! Will we have buried it in the napkin of a narrow, hot-house religious life?

The Mother of God is so imitable that we are apt to believe her way of life unattainable. Mary's example reaches down so intimately into the life of every woman, that we simply cannot grasp the fact. It is the unhappy paradox of a jaded generation with a chromium mental outlook. We are stirred by a Brooklyn boy bearing the Christ into an African bush; and we rally to the story of some nun bearing the good news of the Gospel to tormented prisoners in some remote concentration camp. Such "colorful" Christ-bearers can shake our spiritual lethargy without any permanent injury to the lethargy. The quiet self-sacrifice of the Blessed Virgin Mary is another thing! Her physical bearing of the Son of God is her unique privilege, because of which we have all hailed her as blessed these two thousand years, and will call her blessed for all eternity. Her active and outward Christ-bearing remains far more unique than it should be! Mary's spirit of utter giving is not so much a matter of Scriptural incidents as of Gospel atmosphere. Yet there are specific acts of hers which sound clarion calls to our ennui and to our spiritual provincialism, had we the ears of heart to hear. Her bearing of Christ to Elizabeth is one of them.

Mary had every reason to stay at home. A young girl beginning pregnancy would scarcely be expected to make a difficult and tedious journey through the hill country merely to assist a cousin who had many friends and kinswomen close by to help her. Yet, Mary went; and (we love the endearing human phrase!) she went "with haste." For, Mary knew that she could bring Elizabeth what no one else could bring her: the Christ. The results of Mary's initial act of bearing Christ to others had immediate and amazing results. Elizabeth became a prophetess and co-composer of the tenderest and most universal of prayers. Her son was freed from original sin and made a charming attempt to exult into a separate life of his own. We, with our saving burden of *Pax et bonum!* have an exquisite and peculiar legacy; we do well to remember it was left us to be given away. The giving of the Little Poor Man shook all of society.

There is a second ramification, too. The fatigue which small services can impose, the dull weariness of constant fidelity, take on a real splendor when we remember the young Mary riding

The Heart of Her Giving

wearily through the hill country to bring Love to the house of Elizabeth. The priest whose duties pluck the comfortable flesh of spiritual leisure off the unyielding and saving bone of his prayer has for companion the lovely Mother of God. And the nun whose heart pulls her to the choir and whose work pushes her from it, has her own hill country to travel, and a universe full of cousins. Only a true contemplative can afford to be active, for only the contemplative soul has the Christ to give away.

It was the same when poor little Caesar Augustus blew his trumpets and called the roll of his subjects. Augustus was doing the will of God, for which he has deserved to have his name written in the Gospel, the only pity being that the unfortunate man supposed that he was doing his own will. But what of Mary's plans? We make a fatal blunder if we suppose that our Lady's perfect holiness diluted her woman's nature into some sort of neuter compound. Grace builds on nature, and holiness perfects it. This was certainly patent in Mary, the flower of holiness and the triumph of grace. Her familiarity with the Scriptures made her cognizant of the birthplace of her Son: Bethlehem. Yet she had no notion of how this Scripture was to be fulfilled. So she proved herself again the perfect contemplative, going quietly about the usual and contentedly leaving the unusual to God.

And what was the usual those days? What *could* it be, but the happy hours of singing softly to herself as her slim young fingers worked at the loom and her quick feet beat out a rhythm borrowed from the fountainhead of song beneath her heart! There must be swathing bands for small limbs, dainty coverlets, and soft little sheets. Mary was the most womanly of all women and of all times, and she had exquisite experience of a young mother's joy as she fashioned tiny garments and waited to see the face of her Child. All the joy of motherhood found its perfect fulfilment in hers. Yet she alone of mothers knew what her Child would be: the little Son who would not resemble Joseph.

If the mother of any child awaits her appointed hour like the stretch of a song, what was the waiting of the young Mother of God as she looked with love on the dainty little piles of His garments which her hands had fashioned, as she listened to the quick movements of Joseph in the workshop, watching the happy nimbleness of his fingers and seeing the humble, worshipful love in his dark eyes! This was her little home, and everything in it was arranged with an exquisiteness which must remain peculiar to the Immaculate Virgin Mary. Soon the Savior of the world would lie in this crib which Joseph had planed and modelled and caressed with his calloused hands so many times in past weeks and months. But "there went forth a decree from Caesar Augustus". And in one moment, all her woman's plans were shattered, all a young mothers immediate world collapsed. Only a heartless dullard or a great fool could suppose it cost Mary nothing to leave all those "little things" so inexpressibly dear to a woman and particularly to a very young expectant mother.

For Mary, the Scripture was to be fulfilled, not by a dire and sublime intervention of God, but just as our own de tinies are fulfilled, by the often irksome, sometimes arrogant, frequently unworthy actions of others. And "Joseph also went from Galilee out of the town of Nazareth into ... the town of David, which is called Bethlehem, to register together with Mary his espoused wife, who was with Child."

What infinite woman's pathos is caught up in that brief phrase: "Out of the city of Nazareth!" Out of the warm and ineffable haven her love had prepared for His coming, into the weariness of a long journey on rough roads in winter. Out of the dear familiar world of loom and spindle, into a strange and crowded city, with no thought of the tender luggage her mother's heart longed to take. For her, there was only the sturdy little ass, more famous for endurance than for comfort; and for Joseph, the uneven road beneath his feet. Only the swathing bands could be carried along—clasped, who would dare doubt it, beneath her cloak, against her heart.

So Mary became the Christ-bearer anew. Not to her friends and relatives this time; time enough for them to know of the Love she bore, later on. Now she would bear Him to the humblest and poorest. The shepherds keeping their flocks on the Judean hills knew nothing of how shortly their whole lives would be refashioned. Mary bore the Christ to unlovely, clamorous Bethlehem, just as she still bears Him to our atom-splintering age and to the screaming traffic of our over-crowded lives. And the purpose is the same. "The shepherds returned, glorifying and praising God." Mary had made them contemplatives and saints. It is what she purposes to make of us all, as she continues to give her Son away down through the centuries, contemplatives of the cloister or of the classroom, saints of the scriptorium or of the television stage. We love to call her: Mediatrix of all Graces. The young Mother who left a precious world of "little things" to bear Christ Jesus to the unlovely and the unknowing was the Mediatrix who won from the small Savior the grace of sainthood for the shepherds. Her first act after His birth is profoundly significant. We are not told that she clasped Him at once to her own heart. The Gospel is uncompromising: "She wrapped Him in swaddling clothes and laid Him in a manger." After His birth, she would do as she had done when His physical life was still hers, she would give Him away. She laid Him down in the manger, as if to signify that her one office was to bear Him to all the world, as if she would lay Him on the altar of the universe. And her perfect renunciation of all that was hers, of what we are so fond of calling "one's rights," set a star in the heavens. Three men, afar off, saw the star. Mary had borne the Christ far beyond the confines of Bethlehem.

There would be more journeys for God's Mother. Her gift of God would find, even in her own death, merely a new beginning. One more signal act of her giving, though, stands out in bold relief in the infancy of the Man-God: that poignant episode which has given Mary a right to the sorrowful title, Queen of Refugees. The flight into Egypt has been falsely handed down to us by art and apocrypha. It was no vacation jaunt which the little Family took into the strange and terrifying pagan land, with frequent pauses under convenient date palms, and the Holy Child busying Himself with the working of charming and useless miracles. Oh, no! Every wearisome mile of the three hundred and more they traveled to the dubious safety of a heathen land was marked with sweat and pain and anxiety. Imagine the sorrow of tender-hearted Joseph to awaken his beloved Mary and the Divine Child in the middle of the night and bid them rise and leave the little home without ceremony! And what of the new heartache for Mary? Any mother would be completely chagrined at a command to set out traveling at midnight with a very young child, with no time to pack the things a woman considers absolutely essential to a journey, no time to reason or even to reflect—time only to give.

Naturally speaking, the commanded journey must have seemed a flight from evil into evil. Herod and his gangsters were a proximate threat, and instinctively the young Mother must have clasped her Baby closer to her heart. But Egypt? The very name conjured up a thousand fears … exotic pagan land of blistering desert and hard heathen hearts where they would be utterly friendless, stranded, insulated by custom and peninsulated by tongue. Yet they rose up quickly, roused the sleepy little ass, and

The Heart of Her Giving

were off to give Christ to the land that had never heard His name nor knew a prophecy of His coming. We do well to remember that Mary's adamantine faith is a comment on her utter womanliness, not its negation. Had she not felt her young heart twist within her at leaving her little home once more, at spiriting her Almighty Son away like a criminal, her faith would not be the marvel which that same Son would later laud as her truer claim to blessedness than her divine Maternity. In her heart, so versed in the prophecies, must have whispered a dark rumor of the day she would not be able to spirit Him away, when He would indeed die a criminal's death on a gibbet of shame.

And the Holy Child, remember, was a child! Not an impassive adult masquerading in baby flesh, but a truly (if voluntarily) helpless and weak little child. He was not accustomed to being suddenly taken up out of His midnight sleep. He must have cried. Surely, in that hour, her own soul a sword did pierce, and Mary heard even then a later and far more terrible cry: "My God, *my God, why have You forsaken Me?*" (Mt 27:46; cf. Ps 22:2).

But under all the busy horde of little fears racing in her woman's heart was the wonderful peace that characterized Mary as the greatest of contemplatives and also that joyous willingness to serve that characterized all her actions and made them fecund with salvation. It was to be so all her life. Egypt would forever claim a singular dignity among the nations, for the small Christ had breathed its air and run on its flat sands and learned some of its strange tongue with a child's astonishing aptitude. Egypt remains sacred among the lands because Christ was there. And Mary bore Him to Egypt. Even then, symbolically, she bore Him to all the world languishing in pagan vice and sorrowing in a desert of unbelief.

Mary bore the Christ to Egypt, but at what cost to her own tender mother's heart, at what price of comfort and security, at what toll of exhaustion and anxiety! Small wonder that an adult Christ would gently correct that dear and nameless woman to whom every reader of the Gospel is kin and friend: "Rather, blessed are they who hear the word of God and keep it" (Lk 11:28). It was Mary's faith that bore Him in her soul in a sense just as real and even more perfect (we have the word of Truth itself) than her virginal body bore Him in the womb. Yet that word *keep* has a profounder significance than we grasp at first attendance.

If to "hear the word of God and keep it" means to observe it in oneself, there is also another sublime meaning in the term—that piercing and stupendous paradox to which we have alluded before. To keep, in Heaven's synomenclature, is to give away. Mary kept the Word of God because her life of sacrifice uttered it everywhere, whether she carried the Word to Bethlehem or to Egypt; whether she bore It to the aching yearning of lonely old Simeon or back from Jerusalem's doctoral congress to Nazareth, her heart pierced with the new oblation of *His Father's business,* whether she laid her Christ in a manger with her hands, or on the Cross with her soul's acceptance. No one ever possessed the Christ as Mary did and does, for no creature ever so completely gave Him away.

Chesterton has written of the "holy topsyturvydom" of holiness, and he has written well, choosing the same vehicle of paradox for which Christ showed such predilection. To lose one's life is to save it. Poverty is the only wealth. To bear the Christ everywhere is to keep the Word of God in the only secure mode of possession. Perhaps that is our Lady's first message to us all.

It is in the world's darkest season that the April of her compassion puts up its glad shoots and sends out its birdsong of hope. And the best honor we pay her is our emulation of this most imitable of all those saints of whom she is the lovely Queen. The quiet and constant giving which was Mary's vocation is the vocation of every Franciscan, and the challenge which might set the world ringing again with *Pax et bonum!* Without any trumpeting, Mary accomplished more than any other creature ever did or will acomplish. The few signal incidents in her life upon which we have dwelt are the merest handful out of a life that brimmed with giving, until the day when she stood under a dark Cross and gave her Son away to all the ungrateful and errant souls who then became her children by the most unfair exchange the world has ever witnessed. It was a sorry bargain for the Mother of God who became the Mother of men, but it was the birthday of hope for the whole unlovely lot of us who are her children.

V

Freedom from Surfeit

SATURDAY NIGHT IN THE MONASTERY is quite unmistakable. Even a postulant of only a few months would never confuse it with a Thursday night. But about this particular Saturday night, there was something special besides. It had an air about it, a fragrance of preparation beyond what every imminent Sunday demands.

I walked to the front of the choir to begin the Stations of the Cross and glanced at Sister Beatrice's bare foot moving expertly along the organ pedals. It is, I reflected, a wonderful boon that an organist be delivered out of the bonds of shoes. This was obviously no ordinary processional Sister Beatrice was practising. It soared and rejoiced in vast *crescendos*; it recounted and recalled on *pianissimos*. I went down the Stations, finding the triumphant thing she was playing very effective background for the Way of the Cross. For He fell, and He bled, and He died; but all the time He knew what He would do on the third day. Here, too, was the explanation of an enclosed life of penance, I thought. Penance can get very penitential at times, but it always knows where it is going. It also will have its third day.

When I left the choir, I stood for a moment looking out on our Lady's patio where the monastery cat was proudly taking her three new kittens for an evening stroll. The sound of flutes drifted out of the novitiate, and I strained to hear through the open windows the slap-slap of bare young feet marking out the rhythm of an intricate piece, as fingers flew up and down the flutes. Everyone in a monastery is tired on Saturday night. It is the finale of a day even more filled with work than others. Yet, the novices were practising enthusiastically in this treasured small span of free time between collation and Compline, and for the same reason that set off everything about this Saturday night as unusual. We were preparing for the former novice mistress' golden jubilee. And it was going to be, we were determined, a tremendous affair.

The question those outside the wall might want to pose is: what constitutes a tremendous affair in a cloister?

Now, if some persons cannot see the forest for the trees, others cannot see the joy for the tinsel. Before the race of street-cleaners became extinct, there were white-coated men who went along with huge brushes, uncluttering the avenues of debris. Sometimes it appears that what many of us need is a big spiritual brush to unclutter our lives.

If all the neon lights stopped blinking for half an hour, all the TV sets went dead, all the shoppers stopped shoving and auto horns ceased honking, and everyone fell silent for a while, a new prophet might rise up with an old message: "Behold, your redemption is at hand!" (Lk 21:28). Not that neon lights, auto horns, TV sets, and more especially shoppers, are not God's creatures. It is only that we sometimes forget that they *are*. It is always difficult to remember important things in the midst of clutter and noise. For, whereas all creation is shouting that our redemption is ever at hand, its shout is a cry of silence. It will not compete with noise. Or, if creation writes its message in sun on grass or stars on skies, we can still bury the communication under the small clutter and large surfeit of things. The lack of clutter and the freedom from surfeit fall into sharp relief when a tremendous affair appears on a monastic agenda.

Not every nun lives to celebrate her golden jubilee; when one does, the rest of us get quite excited about it. And it is the little accidentals which provide the happy excitement. The jubilee itself, the fiftieth milestone, is an affair of the soul, even of the inner court of the soul, where dwells something of the tranquillity of God. Given this interior cloister, pledged by vow to remain forever a stranger to material surfeit, one can afford to get excited about the small accessories of jubilee joy.

There must be a banquet, of course; but a banquet rather less complicated than most banquets. The jubilarian' stainless steel fork and small knife (equally suitable for table use or for peeling turnips when on KP) will probably get an extra rub or two to make them shine for the occasion. And if her wooden spoon is sufficiently worn from fifty years of soup-ing, it may be considered advisable by the higher authorities to present her with a new wooden spoon. The refectorian will not have to flip through the pages of her Emily Post for reassurance about which fork is laid out first. One stainless steel fork and one wooden spoon make for a delightfully uncomplicated existence.

The menu will present only minor problems for the cook. Everyone knows that peas from the cloister garden constitute the *pièce de résistance* for a jubilee dinner. Unless, of course, Mother Vicaress can persuade her little asparagus plot in back of the shed to produce a full family portion for the great day. And there will be a cake. No ordinary cake, but a real *chef d'oeuvre* on which Sister Cook will expend her full artistic powers. For such festivities as Christmas or Easter, there will be a cake, but always chastely devoid of icing. The monastic customary, however, is at pains to specify that a nun's golden jubilee cake may have frosting. I have always thought this quaint privilege redolent of the simple joy which characterized St. Francis and St. Clare. Small austerities, such as unfrosted cakes, detail the reach of penance even into festivities. But fifty years of prayer and penance qualify a nun to have icing on her cake. Liberated from meat by our rule of abstinence, we are perhaps better prepared than others to appreciate cake. Fifty years of unfrosted cakes condition a nun to appreciate icing.

Is there not a major point in such minor monastic matters? Our lives on every level can get so thick with frosting that we not only never reach the cake, but even grow to loathe the icing. Too much of everything equips us quite perfectly to enjoy nothing. The simple pleasures of a monastery jubilee are not so much a matter of naiveté as of that common sense which is so uncommon. We cannot wallow in pleasures without losing the vision of joy. When pleasures are spare and spaced, they are fingers pointing the path not *to* joy but *from* joy. For evanescent pleasures do not supply for, but flow out of abiding interior joy. If we do not find our true joy in the Lord, then our pleasures have no roots. After a time, they bore us. In the end, we shall hate them and quite possibly ourselves along with them. There remains always the inverse ratio of mulitplying pleasures to diminishing joy.

Everyone will wear her very best apparel for the golden jubilee. That is to say, each nun will sponge her habit with all the vigor she can muster. Some intrepid souls will even take time to press their habits; everyone will press her veil. That will constitute formal full dress for the guests. And no one will have to worry whether another guest may have copied her gown, for the simple reason that all the guests at this celebration make a practice of copying one another's gowns.

As for the jubilarian herself, she will be resplendent in a new cord, a new veil, and even a new habit. Most golden jubiliarians protest vehemently about the new habit: "I haven't enough time left to wear out another habit." The old nun is usually reassured by the abbess: "Dear, you can wear it to heaven." I remember Blessed Margaret Clitherow busy in prison stitching herself a new white gown for her imminent martyrdom. It is very significant that Poor Clares will patch and darn and mend for fifty years. Then, there must be a new habit. The jubilarian is approaching the greatest day in her life and being outfitted for it before hand.

It may be that one has to be freed from the fetters of changing and tyrannical styles to arrive at a schooled appreciation of the beauty of a superbly-darned habit or the awe-inspiring qualities of a new one.

There must be gifts for a golden jubilarian. Even if we were not delivered from the shopping jungles, there would be very little to shop for. What does one give a Poor Clare on her fiftieth wedding anniversary? She probably needs a new apron, daily manual labor taking the sad toll it does of aprons. And a novice is struck down by the happy inspiration that maybe it could be a *green* apron because, dear Mother Abbess, you know it is her favorite color. And would it be too singular to make the pocket yellow because it is for a golden jubilee? The abbess pronounces judgment on the case. There will be a green apron with a yellow pocket. And there are two ways of viewing such a gift: either you think this is all childish nonsense, or you think it is a vital demonstration of how nothing is small to love. If you take the latter stand, you may come to understand that a green apron with a yellow pocket symbolizes a whole host of major realities: love that is tender, poverty that is gay, simplicity that is secure beyond the reaches of cynicism.

Someone will stitch a new breviary cover for the jubilarian, and each ribbon marker will be selected with as much or perhaps more care than the purchaser at Tiffany's shows as he bends over velvet ring cases.

One of the novice mistress' "alumnae" is breathless over her success in modelling a statue of our Blessed Mother as a jubilee gift. And another recent graduate from the novitiate, and one of our more promising carpenters, is making a wooden shrine for the statue. We all confidently expect our jubilarian to collapse with appreciation before such a triumph of a surprise.

The gifts pile high. And in each one are the sacrifices of time and effort loving hands have made to get these things done. Is there a fur at Peck & Peck to compare with the least of them?

All this is in the air of Saturday night before a jubilee. Someone is in the chapter room, singing over the plain-song propers of the Mass in a final private rehearsal. The cook gives a final fond glance at her cake and spells out the frosted lettering just once more: "Our beloved bride!" Sister Anne pulls the last basting thread out of the jubilarian's new habit. Sister Beatrice makes one final survey of the music books piled at each singer's place, and mentally ticks off the ceremonies again: processional—Psalm—renewal of vows—Mass—motet—postlude—recessional. Yes, everything is ready. The yellow satin ribbons, carefully saved from funeral bouquets donated for years past, hang in graceful arcs over the novitiate door, the refectory walls, across the chapter room. And who wants decorations finer than these?

Maybe a tremendous affair in a monastery has a secret to reveal to those who have too much of everything and so little of satisfaction. Joy is a fragile, shining thing. It cannot shoulder its way out of clutter. It gags on surfeit. But it triumphs when surfeit has burst asunder. It endures when all the clutter has fallen to dust.

VI

Poetry and the Contemplative

U NDOUBTEDLY, it was the immediate and astonishing success attending the first publications of Father Louis Merton that occasioned so intense a focussing of the public eye upon the canonical contemplative life in the United States. The qualifying adjective, "canonical," is used with stress of purpose here, as distinguishing from other religious and other Christians, those religious men and women who live in cloisters and devote themselves to what are very aptly called the works of the contemplative life. While canonical contemplatives are given a unique and rare vocation by God, they are not necessarily the greatest theological contemplatives. The greatest contemplative *per se* within the orbit of your own experience may quite possibly be your bus-driver. Such matters are God's secrets, jealously guarded to be part of our revelatory joy on the day of the general judgment.

Contemplation is a state of soul, not a state of life. There is a contemplative state of life which, of itself, is more conducive to contemplation than any other given state. Once these simple definitions are made, we have the key to the verbal (and invariably verbose) enigmas posed by persons who have immediately disqualified themselves to be contemplatives at all, by the fact of their making absurd comparisons in disfavor of the contemplative state of life.

Like Chaucer's scribe, they "glosen up and down," and present a long-suffering reading public with the embarrassing information that Christ once made an unfortunate remark. When He declared that Mary had chosen the better part, He did not wish to be taken literally, insist such exegetes. Now the only thing more rash than refusing to accept a statement of Christ would be attempting to defend it. And so contemplatives in cloisters prefer not to be so rash. They are not interested—to put it very crudely—in trying to prove that they are better than others for the simple reason that they are sure they are not as good.

Who are called to be canonical contemplatives in cloisters? Very few. Who are called to be theological contemplatives? All. Startling as it may sound to ears abused by discourses on such bizarre subjects as "Contemplation vs. Poetry," that statement is very true. We all look toward heaven, our fatherland. And there is no one in heaven, angel or saint, who is not a contemplative. There never will be. Our destiny is not active service, but contemplation, though on earth some souls are best prepared for celestial contemplation by an active apostolate, while others are called to begin directly their eternal personal fulfillment.

Poetry and the Contemplative

All of this is much easier to grasp than we realize at first shock, having been too long accustomed to futile debate on a subject admitting no debate. If there is one thing wholly unpalatable to the liveliest imagination, it is the picture of any saint caviling about one state of life being superior to another.

Before the release of Father Louis Merton's first slender and excellent volume of poetry, *Thirty Poems*, J. Catholic Publique (J. C. P.) was largely content to let contemplation alone. He knew in a vague sort of way that the contemplative state of life was a good idea—for others. And he was glad in a nebulous fashion that some men and women lived in cloisters and went all-out for prayer and penance. He sensed in an equally vague sort of way that he was probably benefited by the lives of these strange men who wrapped themselves up in cowls and silence, by these mysterious women who went barefoot and got up in the middle of the night to pray—for him. That was that. Now, suddenly, here was a young man in a cloister writing authentic poetry of marvelous beauty and tremendous impact on subjects J. C. P. could understand and which moved him profoundly.

When the young monk's autobiography, *The Seven Storey Mountain*, was released, contemplative life in the cloister became too vivid, too proximate to be relegated any longer to the dusty upper shelves of Catholic mentality. Everywhere, hearts leaped up in response to the compelling warmth of this gifted poet "buried" in his cloister. It is unfortunate that, after the first conflagration of enthusiasm began to settle down into healthy flames, a phalanx of pseudopedants began peering into this matter of a contemplative writing poetry and coming up with some astonishing pronouncements. A true contemplative, they sorrowfully declared, could not be expected to write consistently good poetry.

Even more unfortunately, some of the subsequent writing of Father Louis seemed to uphold these conclusions. Poems became less flamingly beautiful, more strident in tone, inspiration sometimes seeming to be suffocated by style. Subject matter grew too highly-personalized at times, to the extent of excluding or confusing his audience. Those of us who greatly admire and delight in God's gift of song so superbly manifest in Father Louis Merton, feel that the dwindling of his singing is not a matter in the domain of forensics. Sometimes a contemplative religious stops writing poetry for a time simply because song demands pause as well as quaver. Sometimes he has the time to turn out prose, but none for the painstaking perfecting of a poem. Sometimes, like Belloc, a poet "leaves his native land" of poetry in favor of prose for a reason among many reasons as multiple as they are worthy. Belloc felt that prose was the medium of the warrior he had pledged himself to be for God and Holy Church. And although he only hinted at the pain of this sacrifice, Eleanor Belloc Jebb made it evident when she said to this writer: "My father hopes to be remembered as a poet."

Precisely where the nonsense that perfect contemplation (in the relative sense, of course) and good poetry are not compatible began is not easy to say. It is more like a miasma rising out of the swampy talk of persons who are neither contemplatives nor poets. The pity is, that many sincerely religious souls and certain very fine poets appear to subscribe to the idea or at least to give it an attention it in no way deserves. The fact that so many priests and nuns (and nuns carry the field here, we do sorrowfully admit!) write very bad poetry, narrow in compass, piously personalized, and maddeningly repetitious in theme, has probably had much to do with tilting opinion against a contemplative religious as a poet for the world. Yet just here we find the pulse of this whole *non sequitur.*

Poetry and the Contemplative

If a contemplative nun loses contact with humanity in her poetry, it proves not that she is growing more absorbed in God, but that *she is failing in her contemplative vocation.* A contemplative has as much right to write bad poetry as any other poet. It is when her poetry is *consistently* written on a God-and-me plane that leaves no foothold for anyone else, that we stir uneasily not so much for her failure to be a good poet as for her failure to be a true contemplative.

The witches' tales of ivory-tower contemplatives deserved exploding long ago, yet they continue to thrive. There has never been an ivory-tower contemplative; for, the contemplative nun who does not bear the whole torn, suffering, lonely world in her heart is no contemplative at all. To be absorbed in God is to be conscious of humanity in the most sublime way of all. To forget everything in a rapt gaze on Love itself, is the most perfect way to remember and to love. The life of contemplation is a life of holocaust precisely because the contemplative gives herself utterly to God and *thus*, in the most perfect manner possible, to men. Her cloistered life is a failure if it does not make her more compassionate than the tenderest of natural mothers. Thus it was that St. Clare could write: "And if a mother love and nurture her daughter according to the flesh, how much the more ought a Sister to love and nurture her Sister according to the spirit?" And "her Sister" for Clare meant not only her Sisters in religion, but souls everywhere, as is obvious from her own life.

A cloistered contemplative who loses contact with humanity "outside" in the sense of nestling down into a cozy dedication to perfection for perfection's sake is the most tragic of failures. It is only natural that she should write bad poetry, narrow poetry, pietistic poetry. If it is very true that the contemplative must live, in one sense, as though only God and her soul existed, the other sense or facet of the same splendrous truth is that, as touched on above, she forgets in order to remember. Finding God by losing creatures is to find all creatures in Him. That is the secret of the vast, heartbreaking and heartaching love of the real contemplative for all men. Not humanity, a great shapeless lump of it. No, but all men, each man. There is no room in cloisters for souls of less than universal capacities. And if the girl (or man) happens to be a poet, then she is blessed in having a vocation which, *more than any other*, should assist her to write poetry of universal impact and significance.

Franciscans have always sung. Song is their heritage. A Franciscan contemplative is not someone called to disclaim the heritage of all contemplative Franciscans. It is only in surrendering all things that we own everything. And it is only by leaving the world that we are sufficiently purified to take the whole world to our hearts. Given the same talent, the same sensitive awareness, the same capacity for intense feeling, a contemplative should write more excellent poetry, more universally appealing poetry, more authentically beautiful poetry than a non-contemplative. She is closer to the Source of all genuine inspiration. Every detail of her life is completely subjected to and entrusted to the Holy Spirit without Whom, whether the poet knows it or not, no great poem has ever been or ever will be written. Her unique vocation is to be *entirely* dedicated to the service of mankind because she is utterly given to God. Because her every breath and action are directed without any intermediary activity as such to the Most Holy Trinity, she is perfectly attuned to the vast hum of creation, to the song of its joy and the groan of its anguish. This is not to say that contemplative poets always write splendrous songs. But when they do not, it is the fault of their poetry and never the praise of their contemplation. In fact, if a contemplative poet consistently writes

Poetry and the Contemplative

narrow, over-personalized poems, we may fear for her contemplation.

It is noteworthy and deeply significant that poor, unlettered persons are often quick to grasp the point which pedants miss. Those who reduce the contemplative to the status of a hothouse flower not to be exposed to the blasts of other men's anguish and ecstasy, talk sheer nonsense. Why is there always a stream of suffering humanity through the outer gates of a cloister, except that these people have the intuitive wisdom which the professionally learned often lack? These "little people" will never be asked to propose their theories of contemplation and poetry on anyone's lecture platform, nor will they be invited to defend the validity of the contemplative state of life in a world needing active charity. Yet, without any brilliant reasoning on the subjects, they *know* with the perfect instinct of a Christian sufferer that here, in this silent cloister they are immensely loved, their sorrows of tremendous importance, their blessings savored with singing joy.

Why do hundreds of rank-and-file Christians come to divulge the sheerest intimacies of their hearts and souls to a strange, veiled woman behind a grille, save that they sense her perfect compassion for their sorrows and the exquisite tenderness of her love for them? Cloistered contemplatives are made the repositories of tortured secrets whispered to no one else, precisely because suffering brings its own unfailing intuition of where it will be compassionated and healed. These poor of the world, so wise in the ways of the spirit, pour out their tattered little tragedies not only in the surety of receiving loving understanding, but because they know that this is the clinic of all the world, the place where something is likely to be done about their problems. That is why they so often leave a crumpled dollar or some sweaty coins behind them. They so take it for granted that contemplative religious exist for *them*, that they consider it their duty to help feed and clothe their spiritual benefactors. They would be extremely bewildered by the strange talk of persons who say these contemplatives cannot write superb poetry of universal dimensions because they are too engrossed in God to think of humanity.

Persons who should know much better have said that Christ always brought the fruits of His solitary meditation and prayer back to men; and, *therefore,* the cloistered contemplative life cannot be the most perfect state of life since it does not let its followers function in the manner of the Lord. Must we be so crass as to subscribe to the view that service must always be *corporal*, that fruits of prayer must always be *preached*, and that charity must always be *ponderable?* It would be no more absurd to accuse a nurse of not being a professor. There are many diverse modes of bringing the fruits of one's prayer to others, and to remain on the mountain instead of descending from it by no means implies that the solitary keeps all his wares for personal consumption, but only that he dispenses them in a sublimer manner.

A self-centered contemplative is the greatest of all conceivable monstrosities. Since to be engrossed in God is to hear the heartbeat of all His creation, God-centered can never mean humankind-divorced. This sort of a "God-centered" contemplative would indeed qualify for the delicious Irish tag: "a curiosity to God." And a contemplative poet out of touch with humanity would be a curiosity to the Poet in the Trinity, the Holy Spirit.

There is the upper side. And the underside may have some significance, too. This latter is: the *necessity* of poetic expression for a contemplative poet. Now, canonical contemplatives are dedicated to silence and to cloister. There are no seminars for them, no panels, no round-table discussions. But there is still the pressing, painful, driving necessity of poetic utterance for the contemplative poet. When the great poet and prophet, Jeremias, cried out in the ecstatic anguish of his soul: "A! a! a!" (Jer 1:6) he was the precursor of the contemplatives who have felt the solid earth slip and open under them, and groped out for the only possible crutch of articulation: poetry. If it is certainly true that silence is the language of contemplation, it is likewise sure that such silence is fecund with poetry. John of the Cross, in his solitary cell, wrote the most sublime and universal of love songs. Francis of Assisi, nearly blind, sang out the praises of Brother Sun in his incomparable poem, *The Canticle of Creatures*.

There is no resisting the compelling force of the Holy Spirit, given only good will. When He presses the contemplative poet to sing either of her own religious experience that men may share it and be moved by it, or of any subject whatever illuminated by the sure candles of her contemplation or sublimated into a transcendancy of the merely apparent by her love, she will have no rest until the song is sung. The very need, insistent as no other demand quite is, to share her discovery and her experience with others, testifies once again to the universal quality of the contemplative vocation. That there is a piercingly sweet and almost overwhelming sense of personal *relief* when the poem is caught on paper, testifies to it again by the direct argument of the Holy Spirit.

The vocation of the enclosed contemplative cannot be parochial. Necessarily, the field of her apostolate is measured by the circumference of the world—that "small cottage" set on the lawn of her Father's infinitely vast estate, eternity. Her songs, then, must be for the world and every man in it equipped with an intellect to hear them, a sensitive heart to be their sounding-board, and a capacity to bear their message. The contemplative must be the mother of the world. Her poetry must be the food of all the hungry. If she fails in the first office, she cannot succeed in its poetic function. Yet it remains the sublime task of the contemplative poet to be a singing mother for all whose feet are turned toward the mountain at whose peak we shall all hope to sing forever and forever, "Holy! Holy! Holy!" (Is 6:3), being all of us contemplatives forever.

VII

THE SACREDNESS OF THINGS

MY NAVY BLUE DIRNDL didn't show grass stains like the pink or yellow ones of my classmates, so I had the advantage in pulling in the water lilies. We were stretched out, faces down, at the edge of the pool, seeing who could commandeer the most of those lovely fairy floats. And I was winning because I had long arms and because my dark dirndl would stand for more squirming and wriggling on the damp grass at the edge of the pool. I had just got hold of the farthest lily that everyone had wagered could not be captured, when a Sister's voice cut across my triumph. "You're hurting that plant." She sounded like I'd hurt *her*.

I *had* broken the curled edge of the lily, but how was a person to drag it along over the water without breaking it? Anyhow, what was the difference? "It's only a flower," I said in surprise. I got up and dusted off my skirt. I examined the new grass stains on my white canvass sandals, and wished somebody would say something. No one did. So I said, "I'm sorry," feeling about half as old as my fourteen years.

It was picnic day for the staff of *The Rocket*. All the girls who worked on the school paper were there with the Sister Moderator and her companion. And I have wondered whether I was the only one who editorialized to herself that evening about the sacredness of things. I started working off my chagrin at being rebuked before everyone else—and about a water lily! But I progressed to speculating on why a water lily seemed so important a piece of creation to Sister. From that, it was only half a jump to reflection on the way all the Sisters I knew seemed to revere little things. Up till then, I had supposed that not slamming doors, not dragging their feet, not banging down coke bottles, and not scuffing their desks were negative talents Sisters inherited with their religious vocation. Now I began to suspect there might be something more behind it. It might have something to do with reverence.

Our American History class was in the throes of an American Legion oratorical contest that year, and I had lately delivered myself of a dissertation on reverence for the rights of man. I felt I was an authority on the subject by reason of having exhausted my small powers of eloquence on it. Now I started wondering whether I had simply been discoursing on a slogan.

We Americans have a peculiar penchant for slogans. And slogans can be the most effective of all mental anaesthetics. Anyone could select examples almost at random from any chapter of history. Giving a resounding slogan, men will rush into their own destruction, mouthing the motto most of them have probably never bothered to examine. And if wars are most often devised by the avaricious and ambitious, they are often enough fought by those bemused by a slogan.

The Sacredness of Things

Something of this strange tendency to fall spellbound under an often-repeated formula carries over into the soundest declarations men have made, making them less a part of our own working philosophy of life than high-sounding phrases quite unrelated to the practical details of life. One of these, I discovered, could be: reverence for the rights of man.

Now, reverence for the rights of man is, like a soft voice, "an excellent thing in a woman." Or in a man. But the stern fact is, without a reverence for the rights of God, there is no nobility in a reverence for the rights of man. Why? Because without the first, the second is a myth, such stuff as dreams (and not enduring dreams) are made of. Reverence for the rights of God, however, is a very priggish phrase. It smacks of giving a due consideration to someone who apparently has some genuine claims to respect. We shall be happier and much more logical talking of reverence not for the rights of God but for God. Not the just claims of higher authority, but the compelling force of beauty and goodness and love which *is* God. Why should anyone command our reverence for himself or his rights except that he is a splendid and immortal bit of God's craftsmanship, except that he came from God, beautiful, and should be returned to Him so? Each one's right to be revered stems directly from God's right to be worshipped.

When we arrive at that point in our thinking and our praying where an immense reverence overtakes us for the Divine Person Who thought of us from all eternity, created us, sustains us, and loves us, we have gained the proper perspective on the whole hierarchy of creation. We are filled with that blend of awe and love which is reverence, and we begin to see that this God Who made us quite gratuitously—after all, God was under no obligation to create us!—is entitled to have His handiwork reverenced as well as Himself. Here is the fresh wellspring of reverence for all living creatures. And out of it flows the real reverence for the genuine rights of man.

Moving down this hierarchy of values, we come to that reverence for all the furniture of God's world, and realize that His love has appointed us stewards of His creation. One day we shall be asked to give an account of our stewardship from the care of our own and others' immortal souls and bodies right down to our respect for the small furnishings of the universe, the pianos in its parlors, the water lilies in its ponds.

Before I left a hospital in one of our large cities some years ago, I was taken across the street to inspect and admire the new nurses' home. I was delighted at the charm of all its appointments, and even blinked a little at the luxurious comforts of it. We went upstairs, and the matron unlocked the door of an immense room flanked with a grand piano, studded with deep armchairs and couches, lit by sunlight laughing in at a dozen near-ceiling-high windows and spilling across the broad oak floor. "This is the recreation room," she explained, "but it's half-ruined already. Most of my girls are ladies; they like to keep beautiful things beautiful. But others—well, they don't seem to see …" Her voice trailed off. I lifted two question marks of eyebrows, but she didn't expound on her theme. Then, after a few minutes, I began seeing things for myself: the heel and toe scuffs on the bright wastebaskets that had been unfortunate enough to intrude on someone's short-cut to a window. The scratches on armchairs where pointed fingernails had doodled surrealistic designs. The cigarette burns on the piano's lovely finish. I saw more and more traces of our peculiar American brand of vandalism. And I had a painful recollection of the hot resentment I'd felt in my own college days when I read some European's evaluation of us. "Americans," he concluded his observations, "have the culture of goats." I disagree as stoutly as ever I did, but that recreation room would not have been a very stout refutation of his conclusion. It would not have spoken very loudly about reverence.

There are two ways to look at a situation like that, and both can proceed from the same principle. Oddly enough, it is the principle on which the glamour magazines operate: the world was made just for me! That can be understood as meaning that nothing matters except my wishes, my ambitions, my comfort. If it is, there is no reason to reverence the wishes of others. Humility is nonsense. And anything which gets in my way should be promptly kicked out of it. Or, it can mean that the God Who created me as a unique masterpiece of His Love, Who would have died on the Cross to redeem only me, has set me in this world to make its beauty more apparent by my reverence for it, for all the glorious hierarchy in its creation. This is to understand one sense of Hopkins' meaning when he said the Virgin Mary "had this one work to do, let all God's glory through." It is to share in that sublime vocation of hers. It is to be humble and reverent before the miracle of having been created and placed as a special steward over God's household of the universe.

Father Louis Merton has said you can tell a saint by the way he picks up a book. You can discover a lady and a gentleman by the way they close a door or handle their coke bottles, and also by the condition of the books they return to the library. Sometimes it is supposed that if reverence is admitted to have any existence at all outside church doors, then it is something to be pressed in an old-fashioned memory-book of the era of lace jabots. Yet, reverence is as manly a virtue as ever a virtue was.

It was St. Francis of Assisi's sense of reverence that endeared him to everyone who knew him and has endeared him to all ages.

He never thought about reverencing anyone's right, nor even about anyone's having any rights. He was so filled with an awestruck reverence of God Who had created all the loveliness in life that he reverenced every work of His hands whether it was a man or a wildflower or a town. "God," declares the book of Genesis, "looked on His creation, and He saw that it was very good" (Gen 1:31). St. Francis looked on God's creation and saw that it was indeed very good. He moved through all the life like a humble man in a great cathedral, handling its every appointment with exquisite care. And, before long, rough men found their lost gentleness, coarse men retrieved their dignity. Reverence is very contagious because it is a quality as virile as a virus.

Slammed doors, kicked chairs, cigarette-scarred pianos all spell the unlovely biography of the irreverent. And this biography extends from the broken thing to the misused person. Depend on it, the boy who respects his or another's home and its furnishings will also respect his girl. The girl who has a feeling for loveliness and is careful not to deface it is a girl who also reverences her own person. The world was created beautiful, and we are the stewards set here to keep it so. We do not know just when we shall be asked for an account of our stewardship, but we shall certainly be asked. The steward who took care of the small movables of life will be the one most likely to have a good account to give of his reverence for other persons because he will have reverenced the God Who made them and Who is the giver of any rights we have.

In the end, our "rights" reduce to this: being good stewards of the property of God. And His property includes our souls and bodies and all things that are, for all is the work of His hands and all is exceedingly good.

VIII

THE ART OF PRAISE

A CERTAIN PROFESSIONAL CHOIR DIRECTOR gives as a norm his own ratio of blame and praise: Praise your choir once for every ninety-nine times you criticize. Possibly he has a well-disciplined choir, or, at least, a mentally well-corseted choir. It is improbable that he has a joyful choir.

Criticism is a valuable commodity. It is something to be prized, something an intelligent person will seek. Yet, in speaking of criticism, we are careful to qualify it as "constructive." Destructive criticism is already perfectly described. It is destructive. And it can not only destroy initiative and spontaneity; it can also be a singular blight on normal happy human relationships. But, what of this constructive criticism?

If it is constructive, designed to build up rather than to tear down, criticism needs something to build on. And this is where praise becomes an element even of criticism. We seek to build up what is better on what is already good. Finding the good on which to build is the task of human love, and it can be the most rewarding task in the world. Out of much searching comes a glad facility in finding. Sometimes the finding is a revelation, too, as when we discover in the broad noonday of love's eye, that what appeared blameworthy in the twilight of non-understanding, is not only actually blameless, but frequently praiseworthy. And why should what is worthy of praise not be praised?

We get an uneasy feeling about praise sometimes. It tastes very delicious, of course, when spooned up to ourselves. But isn't it a risky business for others? Aren't children spoiled by praise, don't young people have their heads turned by it, and aren't old people addicted to it often enough? Perhaps. But was the fault with the praise or with the people? We ought not be in a great hurry to condemn the seed, if the trouble was in the soil.

On the other hand, sometimes the seed *is* inferior. And this concerns idle praise, insincere praise, lush praise. It is true that to live on chocolate marshmallows is not the way to keep a lean figure and a fit physique; but true praise is nonfattening. It is water, pure and fresh and cleansing; it is bread simple and sustaining. If many heads are turned around by false praise, many hearts are turned down by lack of honest praise. Maybe it is not too extravagant to speculate that the number of spirits wizened for want of loving praise is fifty per cent higher than the number of heads swelled by excess of idle praise.

Praise of God is an art in which the saints all excelled. Praise of their fellows was part of this art; for as our relations with God are, so our relations with people are. St. John minces no words about the man who says he loves God, and yet hates the man down the street. He's a liar, says St. John (cf. 1 Jn 4:20). Two mutually exclusive elements cannot occupy one heart at one time. Love drives out hatred. Hatred is the confession of our inability to love. On a descending scale, enmity of any kind toward any person is an admission of the defectiveness, fatal or remediable, of love.

It is the same with gratitude. To be grateful to God for life and death, joy and sorrow, is to be immediately grateful to our friends whose love embellishes life and sweetens death, doubles our joys and halves our sorrows. You will wait a long time to find the person who is thankless to others for small services singing out his thanks to God for divine servicing of his spirit. In fact, waiting is not recommended, as eternity will close in on that unrewarding vigil.

Clear as the coexistence of love of God and love for those around us is, or as gratitude to God and thanks to those who serve us, carrying over that same logical process into the sphere of praise is often not only not accomplished with facility, but involves a total collapse on the road from premise to conclusion. We shall go along with Bing Crosby who narrates the words of St. Francis on a popular recording, declaring that, "In the morning, every man oughta praise God." Shall we say as sincerely that, "Each day, everybody oughta praise people?"

Our Lord said, "And when you have done all things well, say: 'We are unprofitable servants'" (Lk 17:10). Say it to yourselves, He said. There is no mention of His recommending that we say it to other people. And there is no record that He ever said it to anyone. The Man-God manifested considerably more of human feeling than we sometimes do. And while He personally accepted meekly and humbly blame and criticism of everything He did, still He did not appear to savor it. He uttered very poignant human complaints, too, like: "Where are the nine?" (Lk 17:17) when He had cured ten and been thanked by one; "For which of these do you strike Me?" (Jn 18:23) when He had listed manifestations of His goodness; "Can't you watch one hour with Me?" (Mt 26:40) to His three heavy-lidded friends whom He had taken into the intimacy of His anguish.

And when a centurion said that he understood authority because he had some himself, and that when he said, "Jump!" men jumped; and when he went on to declare that he believed Christ had only to speak one authoritative divine word, and his servant's illness would betake itself out of him, the Lord praised the man. "I have not found such great faith in Israel!" (Mt 8:10). Christ rejoiced. There are those who might worry that it was rather lavish praise, saying this fellow had it all over hundreds or thousands of steady, righteous people; yet one doubts the centurion's head was turned, though it is very likely that his heart was turned in an entirely new direction—toward the kingdom of God.

There was that Canaanite woman, too, that magnificently determined lady who not only refused to retreat into wounded hauteur on being compared with a dog, but who turned the Lord's words back upon Himself to His own evident delight and won the glorious praise the rest of us may well covet: "O woman, great is your faith" (Mt 15:28).

None of us dearly loves to be blamed *all* the time. Even in religious life, this sturdy old method of raising up saints has fallen into public disrepute. Stern criticism is valid and availing only when the dispenser has demonstrated that he also understands how to give a warm word of deserved praise.

The saints knew this well. Even a brief study of the life of St. Francis of Assisi will reveal that he was so wonderfully successful in dealing with people because he did not hesitate to praise what was good in them. His love for people went in a circle, but not the proverbial vicious circle, rather a glorious circle of unending

The Art of Praise

discovery. His love ferretted out the hidden good in the most unlikely human soil. He praised it. And the one praised, often enough some poor derelict who had never been praised before, became happily astonished at the good Francis had discovered was in him. Good discovered became good acknowledged. Good acknowledged and recognized begot more good. And, except in the cases where there was invincible ill will or fatal hardness of heart (those cases which broke Francis' heart), the glorious circle went on turning. It turned out hundreds of happy men. It even turned out quite a few saints.

Praise is an art. When rightly understood and practiced, it is a great spiritual art. We shall spend all our eternity in praising God. To get a little practice on earth for our eternal occupation is surely a reasonable idea. Yet, the praise of God is not so often grouped with matters in which we are determined to acquire more facility. If all eternity has been set aside for saying: "Holy! Holy! Holy!" (Is 6:3) there must be something in it. It must be an inexhaustibly delightful occupation.

The truth is: never to have experienced the delight of simply praising God, asking nothing, desiring nothing, conscious of nothing at the moment except how lovable and praiseworthy is the Lord, is really to have missed your connections in life. It leaves a flatter taste in the soul than that left in the mouth when you have missed the last bus. St. Francis, all the saints, were so happy because they were deeply involved in the happiest of commitments, the unceasing praise of God. They praised God for agreeable things because they were agreeable. They praised God for disagreeable things, because they had faith. Really to believe in God is to know that He is an alert God, always working out our salvation, always planning our good, missing no opportunity to offer us advancement in His kingdom of love. Believing thus, it becomes consequent on mere normal intelligence to praise God for all He does.

We shall never become adept, though, in the praise of God without being apt for the praise of our fellows. And, let us say it again, overripe praise, hollow praise, false praise, do not enter into it at all. These counterfeits have tried to cheapen praise itself, but they should not be allowed to do so. For true praise is too great, too delicate, too much of an art to be confused with the ersatz article.

Sometimes praise does not seem to "come easy," as we say. We all have a talent, more or less highly developed, for seeing the flaws in others. A rent in a garment always stands out in bold relief from the pattern in the whole cloth. One speck of soot on a lovely face will be enough to deflect our eye from the beauty to the soot. A putrescent sore on an arm will command our attention away from the shapeliness and grace of the limb.

In the realm of personality, spirit, character, this is truer still. We will blame one burst of impatience, with no thought for praising sustained patience under a host of annoyances. We are disgusted with flamboyance, never stopping to consider the feeling of inferiority that prompts it, stopping still less to find something to praise in the person whose sense of inferiority took refuge in the flamboyant behavior. If we did, there might be less feeling of inferiority.

"I don't believe in praising people," is a thing said rather often and in a tone to indicate that the utterer is a person of good balance. Doesn't believe in spoiling people. Isn't going to turn their heads. Is above such things as praise. Enough militant disciples of that kind of teacher, spreaders of that sturdy-sounding doctrine, can shout down the counter-idea that praise is a great spiritual art. The mere fact that it is an art indicates it is to be used with

The Art of Praise

discretion and good taste, not be overdone, overbalanced, overstressed, or overfrequent.

Praise and flattery are not only not synonymous, but are really antonymous. We do not flatter God when we spend our eternity telling Him that He is Holy! Holy! Holy! nor when we spend our lives praising His ordering of our lives. No more do we flatter our companions when we tell them that they handled a difficult situation very well, with God's grace, that they sing very charmingly with the voice God gave them, that they really have God's own gift for mending things. It rather staggers the imagination to picture a holy home of Nazareth where our Lord never told His Mother that the bread was really delicious, or St. Joseph that the new wagon was a masterpiece.

The professional choir director quoted might deplore a state of affairs where the director keeps no ninety-nine-to-one ratio of blame and praise, where, in fact, the director goes by no ratio at all. When a piece is shabbily sung, it is called shabby. If someone has not learned to respond to direction, he is corrected. And when an *Introit* is flat, it is criticized as being flat. However, when a Mass is very well done, the director praises the choir for a Mass very well done. And when there is very delicate response to direction of a difficult phrase, the response is cordially praised. There may be some, however, who would think this quite a sensible arrangement.

There is nothing dangerous about flirting with the concept of praise. In fact, it should be courted, wooed, espoused. What is slippery is our false notion about it. Until we have learned rightly to praise the companions of our life, we are not conditioned to praise God, either. As we deal with others, so do we deal with God, however little it may appear so on the surface.

When St. Clare was dying, she addressed her own soul. "Don't be afraid," she said, "you will have for companion on your journey

One Who has created you and sanctified you and loved you as a mother loves." Then she added a final word of praise of her long life's praises of God and creatures: "Be praised, my Lord, for having created me."

Be praised, God, for having created all the mysterious beings with whom we live; praised for their secret goodness and for their more apparent graces; praised for their efforts and strivings; praised for the successes that are often forgotten because of the failures. "Be praised, my Lord, for having created me." Really, it was a very gracious exit line.

IX

CREATIVE SPIRITUAL LEADERSHIP

I F WE ARE GOING TO TALK about creative leadership, we shall first of all want to clarify what we mean by leadership and what we mean by creative. That these are not self-evident terms or even presently readily understandable terms should be obvious from an imposing current witness to creative leadership envisioned as an abolition of leadership, and a transversion of creativity into annihilation. While it is true enough that, theologically and philosophically speaking, annihilation is as great an act as creation, hopefully we do not analogically conceive of our goal in leadership as being equally well attained by annihilation or by creativity!

As God's creativity is to cause to be something that was not, our creativity as superiors who are quite noticeably not divine, is to allow something that is, to become. As a matter of fact, we assume a responsibility to do this by accepting the office of superior. Much has been and is being written and said about the superior as servant. This is so obviously her role that one wonders what all the present excitement is about. Quite evidently, this role, this primary expression of leadership, has been forgotten by some superiors, even perhaps by many superiors, in the past. But why should we squander present time and energy in endlessly denouncing such past forgetfulness? Let us simply remember truth now, and get on with our business. One characteristic of creative leadership is to point a finger at the future rather than to shake a finger at the past.

St. Clare wrote in her Rule more than seven hundred years ago that the abbess must be the handmaid of all the Sisters, not pausing to labor so evident a fact but simply going on to give some particulars which have a very modern ring: the abbess is to behave so affably that the Sisters *can* speak and act toward her as toward one who serves them. That dear realist, Clare of Assisi, who passes so easily from blunt warnings about such un-monastic natural virtues as envy, vainglory, covetousness, and grumbling, to airy reminders that it is no good getting angry or worried about anyone's faults as this merely deals charity a still severer blow—that dear realist had obviously run up against some personalities who were "handmaids" sufficiently formidable to discourage anyone's rendering them personal recognition in this area.

The abbess is supposed to be lovable, for St. Clare envisions a community where Sisters obey a superior because they love her and not because they dread her. This was quite a novel as well as a radical theology of superiorship in Clare's day. And if it remains radical today, it is a great shame that it sometimes remains novel also. The medieval saint makes so much of this point of the lovableness of the superior that she returns to it in her dying Testament, begging her successors that they behave themselves so that the Sisters obey them not from a sense of duty but from love. It's not just the same thing she is saying again, however. You note that whereas in the Rule she does not want any fear or dread of the superior, in the Testament she rules out dutifulness as well. It has got to be a matter of love itself. Who, after all, would want to be loved out of a sense of duty? It would be insulting, really. Any normal superior would rather be loved in spite of herself than because of her office. St. Clare makes quite a point in her brief Rule and Testament of describing the manifestations of this lovableness she so insists upon. She gives us her idea of creative leadership And its present practicability may make us want to pause and clear our throats before the next time we utter that bad word, "medievalism," as an indictment.

Besides the general affability which Clare describes in her Rule and Testament, she underscores an availability rather beyond and considerably more profound than the "let's sit down in the cocktail lounge and talk about salvation history" mentality. St. Clare wants an on-site superior who is "so courteous and affable" (there's that word again) that the Sisters can tell her their troubles and needs, seek her out "at all hours" with serene trust and on any account—their own or their Sisters'. This last point is particularly arresting, considering again that this is a medieval abbess delineating the characteristics of the creative superior as she conceived those characteristics in about 1250, not a 1970 progressive-with-a-message.

Clare did not favor isolationism in community. Each of her nuns was supposed to notice that there were other nuns around. And she called them Sisters, which was quite original in her day. She favored co-responsibility quite a while before the 1969 synod of bishops, taking for granted that the abbess was not to be the only one concerned for the good of the community, but that it belongs to the nature of being Sisters that each has a loving eye for the needs of all the others. Again, there is her famous saying: "And if a mother love and nurture her daughter according to the flesh, how much the more ought a Sister to love and nurture her Sister according to the spirit!" Yes, it does seem she ought. And maybe we ought to be as medieval as modern in some respects. For some medieval foundresses did an imposing amount of clear thinking on community, on sisterliness, on the meaning of humble spiritual leadership which we, their progeny, could do well to ponder.

So, there's affability, availability, accessibility. When we read St. Clare's brief writings and savor the droll confidences given in the process of her canonization, we can conclude that this superior often toned her Sisters down but never dialled them out.

Then, St. Clare insists that the creative spiritual leader be compassionate. There is no hint of a prophylactic detachment from human love, arid sympathy, nor of that artificial austerity which pretends that to be God-oriented is to be creature-disoriented. No, Clare says of the superior: "Let her console the sorrowful. Let her be the last refuge of the troubled." Note, she does not tell the contemplative daughter to work it all out with God, and that human sympathy is for sissies. And she warns that "if the weak do not find comfort at her [the abbess'] hands," they may very well be "overcome by the sadness of despair." Those are quite strong terms from a woman who did not trade on hyperboles or superlatives and was no tragedienne.

Again, she has something very plain and very strong to say about responsibility. For we had better not talk about co-responsibility unless we have understanding of primary responsibility. "Let her who is elected consider of what sort the burden is she has taken upon her and to Whom an account of those entrusted to her is to be rendered." So, Clare will have the superior clearly understand that she has a definite and comprehensive responsibility to a particular group of people, a responsibility which is immeasurably more demanding than counting votes to determine the consensus. She is supposed to create and maintain an atmosphere in which Sisters can best respond to their own call to holiness. Obviously, she can not do this alone. But she is the one most responsible for making it possible for each Sister to contribute her full share in creating and maintaining this atmosphere. She is the one who is particularly responsible for not just allowing, but helping the Sisters, and in every possible way, to realize their own potential.

If I may deliver to any possibly frustrated or depressed superiors some glad tidings out of my own small experience, I beg to announce this finding: Sisters are not as hard on superiors as many dour authors make them out to be. They do not expect perfection in the superior. They are, as a matter of fact, quite ready to pass over the most obvious faults and failures in the superior as long as they know she loves them and would do anything in the world for them, and is herself struggling along with them to "walk before God and be perfect"(Gen 17:1), and having just as hard a time as they with this quite exacting but certainly thrilling divine program. Isn't it, after all, singularly exhilarating to have been asked by a God Who has witnessed all ones past performances, to be perfect as He is perfect! (cf. Mt 5:48) But that is an aside of sorts. The point I was making is that Sisters will sooner forgive the faults of the warm hearted than the "perfection" of the cold-hearted. At least that is my personal observation. It is not faults that alienate people, it is phoniness. And may it always alienate them, for it is nothing to make friends with.

Now, if the superior is set to create and to make it possible for the Sisters to help create an atmosphere suited to the response to a divine call to holiness, this atmosphere will have to be one of real human living. For the only way a human being can be holy is by being a holy human being. I believe one of the more heartening signs of our times is the accent on humanness. For one of our tiredest heresies is the proposal that the less human we are, the more spiritual we are. Another aside I am tempted to develop here is a reflection on how we describe only one type of behavior as inhuman. We never attribute that dread adjective to the weak, but only to the cruel. But I had better get on with what I was saying, which is that dehumanized spirituality is no longer a very popular goal. This is all to the good. However, we shall want to be sure when we talk enthusiastically about the present accent on real human living in religious life that the qualifying "real" is not underplayed. It needs rather to be underscored.

Certainly, we would evince a genuine poverty of thought to equate real human living with ease. On the other hand, there is evidently a direct ratio between sacrificial living and real human fulfillment; between poor, obedient living and joy; between ritual and liberty; between the common task and real (as opposed to contrived) individuality. Genuine common living in religious life is not the witness of the club, but of the community. Its real proponents are not bachelor girls, but women consecrated to God as "a living sacrifice holy and pleasing to God." Our blessed Lord emptied Himself, taking the form of a servant. And no one yet has ever been fulfilled by any other process than *kenosis*.

Beginning with the Old Testament, history affords us a widescreen testimony to the truth of the binding and liberating power of sacrifice. It binds the individuals in a community together, and it liberates both individuals and the community as such into the true and beautiful expression of self-ness which is what God envisioned when He saw that each of His creations was very good. History shouts at us that self-ness is not a synonym but an antonym for selfishness. May we have ears to hear! Just as nothing so surely situates persons in isolationism as establishing a mystique of ease and a cult of comfort, so does nothing so surely both promote and express genuine community as sacrificial action, whether liturgical or domestic. This generation feels it has come upon the glorious new discovery that the world is good. It is indeed a glorious discovery, but not a new one. St. Francis, for one, discovered this in the thirteenth century. But if joyous Francis owned the world, it was precisely because he never tried to lease it.

It is essential that the creative superior be a living reminder that our situation in time is not static but dynamic, our involvement in the world urgent but not ultimate, our service of others indicative rather than determinative, and our earthly life not a land-lease but a pilgrimage. Somewhere or other I recently read that the one good line in a new play whose name I happily can not now recall is the one where a character looks at a plush-plush apartment hotel and remarks: "If there is a God, this is where He lives." I seem to detect a bit of this mentality in some of our experimentation. This would be only mildly disturbing if it pertained to the kind of luxuriousness that keeps periodically turning up in history until a new prophet-saint arrives on the scene to denounce it and expunge it from the local roster. What is deeply disturbing is that we are sometimes uttering brave and even flaming words about identifying with the poor at the same time that we are rewriting just this kind of past history. But that is another small aside from the large issue, which is real human living and the sacrificial element that is one of the most unfailing preservatives of that "real" in human living.

The material poverty and inconvenience just alluded to is but a minor facet of the idea, but I do think it is a facet. Do any of us lack personal experience to remind us that the poorest communities are usually the happiest? Nothing bores like surfeit; nothing divides like ease.

If it is true—and it is!—that the religious community does not rightly understand its vocation unless it sees itself as part of the whole ecclesial community, the cosmic community, it is equally true (because it is the same truth turned around) that the religious community will be to the ecclesial community and the cosmic community only what it is to itself and in itself. The creative leader will want to accent this to her Sisters so that they can accent it to one another. Not verbally. Just vitally! We shall be to the Church and to the world only what we are to each other, no more and no less. And what we are to each other will inevitably serve the Church and the world.

Every superior is called to be a prophet. Perhaps we could even say that this is her highest creative service in allowing and assisting others to realize their potential, and release their own creative energies. Now that we are all nicely educated to understand that the prophet is not the one who foretells the future so much as the one who says something about the present, the creative superior's prophet role becomes not only clear but uncomfortable. Jeremiah would doubtless have had a much higher popularity rating if he had limited his observations to a pleasant, "*Shalom!*" It is so much easier to say "*Shalom*" than to say "Do penance, or you shall all perish." Of course, it is best of all to prophesy both penance and peace, but we shall have to keep them in that order. And our own efforts to achieve that real human living which has to be rooted in penance and sacrifice give abundant testimony that peace is indeed a consequence of penance performed in love, of sacrifice as a choice of lifestyle rather than just a choice among things.

Obviously, obedience is the profoundest expression of sacrifice. And maybe one of the biggest mistakes that eventuated into that maternalism in religious communities which has had us running such high temperatures in recent press years, is that of supposing that obedience is for subjects only. Allow me another aside to interject here another small idea I have been nurturing. It is, that "subjects" is a very poor word substitute for "Sisters" and of itself precipitates a whole theological misconception of what and who a superior is. Subjects are persons ruled over. However, a servant does not rule. We need to get rid of the monarchical connotations of "subject." And if we begin by getting rid of the term "subject," we may be already better equipped to understand that the superior, as servant, is the first "abject in the house of the Lord." Once we establish her as abject, we shall perhaps be less ready to label her "reject."

A creative superior will have to excel in obedience. It is part of her role as prophet. She must obey others' needs at their specified time according to their manner and manifestations. She must respond not just to the insights God gives her, but to those He gives her Sisters. She should obey their true inspirations as well as her own. She ought to be obedient to the very atmosphere she has helped the Sisters to create. For we can never establish a communal *modus vivendi* and then sit back to enjoy it. Life, like love, needs constant tending. Life needs living as love needs loving. This very thing is essential to creative leadership. Charity is a living thing, and, therefore, it is always subject to fracture, disease, enfeeblement, paralysis, atrophy, and death. The prophet is more called to proclaim this truth and to disclaim offenses against this truth than to wear a "LUV" button on her lapel. It is much easier to wave a "LUV" banner at a convention than to tend and nurture love in those thousand subtle ways and by those myriad small services for which womanhood is specifically designed, in which religious women should excel, and to which religious superiors are twice called.

Real human living which the creative superior is called to promote, can never be anything but spiritual, sacrificial, intelligently obedient, and—yes—transcendental. We need not be wary of the word or the concept. The new accent on horizontalism is well placed, for many of us seem to have got a stiffening of the spiritual spine with past concentration on verticalarity. Still, if we adopt a completely horizontal mentality, we are apt to drift off to sleep as concerns genuine spiritual values. After all, the position is very conducive to sleep.

We are most fully human when we are vertical. Yes, we reach out horizontally, but our face is upturned to Heaven. The really lovely paradox is that it is only when our eyes are upon God that we are able to see those around us and recognize their needs. They are, after all, each of them "in the secret of His Face." It is a vital service of creative leadership that it emphasize the essentiality of the transcendental element in real human living. In fact, we could more accurately talk of the transcendental character of full human living than of any transcendental element. The term of our destiny is not on earth. Therefore, we shall never rightly evaluate anything that pertains to earthly existence unless we see it or are attempting to see it from an eternal perspective. And we shall never really live humanly unless we are living spiritually. Certainly we shall never have a religious community that abounds in warm human affection and mutual concern unless it is a religious community concerned primarily with the kingdom of God. We can properly focus on one another only when we are focused on God. For to be fully human is to share in what is divine: "He has made us partakers of His is divinity" (2 Pet 1:4).

The most natural superior is, therefore, the most supernatural. And real human living must be based on a values system that is transcendental. In these days one need scarcely look far afield to discover what becomes of community when the values system is not transcendental. A group of individual women, each doing her thing, is by no means the same as a community which has a thing to do. To such a community, each Sister brings her own creative contribution, and in it each realizes her creative potential. And a servant of creativity is needed for all this.

There is much more to be said about creative leadership, and others are equipped to say it much better. One can only speak out of one's own experience and with one's own limitations. However, it has been my observation that cloistered living does offer a certain insight into humanity which is sometimes different from that of persons whose professional qualifications doubtless exceed those of the cloistered nun. It's quite predictable, really. We ought to anticipate expertise in human living from those who have chosen to achieve human living in such close quarters. We should expect some special insights into humanity from those who see it at such close range and on such limited acreage. So perhaps these simple thoughts may have some small point to make.

Let me add, then, only a final word about the realization of creativity and about the full expression of human living. We've talked about sacrifice, penance, obedience, transcendentalism. Recently, our Sisters ran up against an example of a truly fulfilled human being. This was a priest in his seventies. At thirty, he'd got drunk. And a series of really devilish events conspired to turn that one mistake into a tragedy for which he was not responsible. He was used by bigots, manipulated by the circumstances they precipitated, and he was deprived of his priestly faculties. He sought help from his bishop who said it was all very sad, but he really could not do anything. He took it to Rome and got put in a file because, though it was all very sad, there was no canon to cover it. He turned to fellow priests who agreed it was all very sad, but they were very busy and there was nothing they could do about it (I am very rejoiced to report that one Franciscan friar did try, desperately, to help.) No priest ever had more provocation to bitterness. He was the example *classique* of being treated as a number and not as a person. So, who could blame him that he wrote such vitriolic articles after he left the Church? Anyone could understand his contempt for the hierarchy. And when he sneered at the Roman Curia, you could only say that, after all, he had really had it.

Only, the fact is, he did not leave the Church, nor did he write vitriolic articles, nor did he sneer. For forty years he lived the obscure life of a workingman. He went to Mass each day. And he persevered in faith. God crowned that faith with exoneration of the past and the restoration of sacerdotal privileges only after forty years, but one can speculate on the interior crowning when one knows that this priest now offers daily Mass with tears that are neither self-pitying nor bitterly scalding. He's just happy. He's just grateful. And he has obviously experienced more personal fulfilment than any of the local protestors, for he is beautiful to behold.

And this is not to say that wrongs don't matter or that protests should never be lodged. It is merely to offer for consideration the evidence of what suffering and silence and unshakable faith can do in the line of creating a fully realized human being. Maybe superiors need to point up these things a little more than some of us sometimes do.

I am scribbling some of this manuscript as I watch at the bedside of a dying Sister of ours. It's my first experience as abbess with death. And somehow all reflections on religious life, on community, on leadership, on creativity are turned upon this one deathbed in this one small cell. I find it a very revealing perspective. Sister has a way of pointing at the ceiling regularly. And when you ask: "What do you see? What is there?" she does not check in with a "vision." She just says: "Joy!" That is the direction to seek for it, if you want to find it on earth.

X

THE SILENCE AND THE SONG

Among the vagaries of the human mind is the propensity for repeating countless times a formula, a phrase, a declaration, without ever really listening to it. This was demonstrated when St. Pius X once asked an assemblage of clergy why holy Church demands that we so often ask the holy Mother of God to pray for us. He received learned answers and verbose opinions. But, in the end, it was the Pontiff himself who smilingly answered the question, "We ask the holy Mother of God to pray for us that we may be made worthy of the promises of Christ!"

In much the same manner, might we ask a group of religious where all happiness and satisfaction lie? We should likely get vague replies about "God" and "heaven." We might receive memorable answers about union with the will of God. It is less probable that we should hear the simple and most precise answer which all

Catholics declare at every Benediction service every day throughout the world. The priest sings out the affirmation that God has given us Bread from heaven; we help swell the great chorus of response, "Having every delight within itself!" How stunning it would be to listen to what we declare and how overwhelming to probe the truth of what we say, so that belief might pass into conviction over that narrow line that separates the mediocre from the saint. The poet, Thomas of Aquin, was thus stunned into singing of the Blessed Sacrament in some of the most magnificent poetry the world has heard. This we are less apt to remember than that he probed the truth with such cherubic comprehensiveness that holy Church has hailed him the Angelic Doctor. Yet, the citizens of a twentieth-century world need nothing so much as a poet to sing a path through its tangled philosophies and its prostitute science. Even religious, dwarfed often enough by their own accomplishments, goaded by ever-increasing demands for new activities, need desperately what the busy world values so little and what St. Thomas prized so intensely: the silence and the song.

World problems today tend to dwarf the individual. In unhappy Europe, men are murdered by block rather than by unit. We have learned to splinter the very atoms of God's creation. Our scientists have peered down the tunneled mysteries of creative substance and won the honor of dismembering it. It is all so vast a field of woe, this world of ours, vast beyond the courage of a man or the hope of a heart.

So it seems from the false perspective of a Godless modern society. But there is quite another perspective, and to gain it brings a shock of sheer joy. It is God's perspective. It is the view of the angel of the schools, St. Thomas. Other men have stood in the panoramic chaos of society and been disheartened to near-despair. They forgot the Blessed Sacrament. St. Thomas stood beside the tabernacle and remembered. And he rejoiced. It is God, God truly present in the world in the Blessed Sacrament Who is vast, overwhelming, infinite, and omnipotent. It is the world which is small. And a world aware that its mighty God has delighted to dwell with the children of men is a very dear world. This is the great good news which it is ours to shout out by our consecrated lives. When we come to comprehend something of the supreme and ineffable gift of God which is Himself, when we say or chant or sing, "*Omne delectamentum in se habentem*," and are convinced of it, then we have established kinship with the poet laureate of the Blessed Sacrament.

All thinking men take a kind of vicarious pride in St. Thomas. We feel his giant intellect as a real "achievement" of God's own pure intelligence. We have a certain gratitude to God for giving this genius to the Church. It is perhaps unfortunate that the master mind of Aquinas has caused history to forget his heart. It is all too easy to think of St. Thomas as a great bulk of reason, a complete network of logic, and a superb mechanism of exposition. This is to miss the man for the mind, the saint for the intellect, the lover for the logician. It was Aquinas the genius who wrote the *Summa Contra Gentiles*. It was Aquinas the saint who lay sleepless in his bed the night before he was to receive his doctorate at the University of Paris, convinced that he was unworthy to bear this title, that his "meager knowledge" did not even fit him to give the expected discourse on the following day. This incomparable genius humbly cried out to God to give him a subject on which to speak to a crowd of men whom history remembers only as figures in the life of St. Thomas! And God heard the simple cry of that pure heart which was to remain childlike to its last beat, and of that magnificent mind which was to pass a final appraisal on the intellectual labors of a lifetime as, "All that I have written seems to me as a little straw."

By force of God-given intelligence, St. Thomas might still claim title to the most competent exposition of the Holy Eucharist ever delineated. But it needed the burning heart of a lover to give us the Office and Mass of the Blessed Sacrament. The poet in Thomas drew virility from intellectual faith; conversely, the intellect of the man was warmed by the poet. It is significant that that most magnificent poem, the Sequence of Corpus Christi, begins with a burning cry of the heart, not with a thrust of logic! If St. Thomas comprehended the mystery of the Eucharist in a measure few men have, it was because Thomas loved the Eucharist. All love, as all goodness, is diffusive of itself. His immense and burning love for the Blessed Sacrament forced him to cry out, "*Lauda Sion, Salvatorem! Lauda ducem et pastorem in hymnis et canticis!*" Not in tracts and expositions did this Angelic Doctor invite men to honor the Blessed Sacrament, not by intellectual feats did Thomas propose that men should worship their Eucharistic Lord, but in a mode and manner accessible to every man with a pulsing heart and a living love—*in hymnis et canticis*! It is no cold empiricist who goes on in that same sublime poem to give directions as to the tonality of this praise, but an enthusiastic lover of the Blessed Sacrament on fire with his message. "*Sit laus plena*," says St. Thomas, "*sit laus sonora!*" like a superlative musician directing his chorus.

We can read in the Sequence of Corpus Christi the life story of the great poet who composed it. The harassed young novice, besought by his tearful mother, coaxed by his sisters, threatened and imprisoned by his brothers, all of them attempting to convince him of his folly in forsaking a brilliant worldly career for the lowly estate of a mendicant friar, pleads his own eloquent and impregnable defense. We find the very heart of Aquinas in that sublimely simple strophe of the sequence, "Here, for empty shadows fled, is reality instead; here, instead of darkness, light." The institution of the Blessed Sacrament brought to the world that substance of reality from which the prophetic words of Christ in His lifetime had cast long shadows incomprehensible to men. It likewise signalled the disappearance of those empty shadows of fame and riches and honors considered as a source of delight—those poor baubles which the family of Aquinas dangled before the saint in their hopeless attempt to make him accept shadows in place of the Sun.

Another chapter in the soul of St. Thomas is discernible in the twelfth strophe of the Sequence of the Blessed Sacrament. The genius who plumbed and expounded divine mysteries as no other man has so manifestly done has a simple remedy for those who find, like the Jews of old, that the mystery of the Eucharist is "a hard saying—and who can bear it?" (Jn 6:61). What escapes the comprehension, says St. Thomas, is the property of faith. Faith leaps to possess what the mind can never understand! This is not only the exposition of faith in the Real Presence; it is likewise the exposition of Thomas' personal philosophy of life. There were many superb intellects in the saint's company at the universities, intellects which ran amuck in the quicksands of pride and mental independence. There were William of St. Amour and his unhappy band of disciples, men whose learning was vast and whose humility was meager, men who discarded whatever was inapprehensible by reason.

It has been well said that the more a man knows, the more he realizes his ignorance. This is manifest in St. Thomas. Wiser far than any of his confreres, he held out the arms of his childlike faith to embrace God's mysteries never to be assimilated by any created intelligence. Every act of faith is of necessity a simultaneous act of humility. The flaming faith of Aquinas shot out its sparks into all the commonplace events of his life. The profound humility of the saint before the unfathomable mystery of the Eucharist was the groundwork of all his hours. Thus we see the great master of learning, puffing along the streets of Bologna in the wake of an exacting lay brother who scolded Thomas for his slow pace and received the charming apologies of his unrecognized companion. We hear the angel of the schools accepting a correction of his pronunciation and contentedly repeating the mistake of his superior without the comment of eyebrows or the significant pause with which a lesser religious would first have demonstrated his superior knowledge before submitting. The childlike humility of Thomas was perhaps his first prerequisite to act as the expositor and the poet of the Eucharist. It is a humble God who lives in the appearance of a disc of bread and submits to that keenest of all insults, the ennui of His ministers and the unconcern of His consecrated own. It needed a humble man to be the gallant knight of the Eucharist. Such a man was Thomas of Aquin.

"*Omne delectamentum. . .*"—yes, all delight to the clean of heart. But what to the unclean? *Omne detrimentum*, we could say. The delectable Bread of Angels can be the awful food of sacrilege. And something of the agonizing Heart of the Christ, outraged, misused and ignored, was the very heart of Thomas. The saint, who witnessed the irreverence and carelessness of so many of the religious of his day for the Sacrament of the Altar, likewise looked with that intense sorrow, which only a great lover can feel, on the wreckage of mental brilliance all about him. Then, as now, the proud and the humble came to the fountains of knowledge—and with what disparate issue! The profound grief, which only a saint can experience at insult to his God, breathes its quiet pain into the Sequence of Corpus Christi: "*Sumunt boni, sumunt mali: sorte tamen inaequali, vitae vel interitus.*" If we understood, with the vision and the love of the Angelic Doctor, that it is the business of each religious to determine the issue of the Blessed Sacrament within himself, we might paraphrase that strophe to a telling, "*Sumunt fervidi, sumunt tepidi!*" or to a, "*Sumunt fideles, sumunt infideles!*" And we could draw a personal conclusion: "*...inaequali...vitae vel mediocritatis!*"

As the splendid poem, "*Lauda Sion,*" draws to its conclusion, we see demonstrated again the subtle interweaving of the masterly intellect and the ardent heart. The great doctor's faith and conviction put out a clean sword of dogma, as he pronounces the indivisible mystery of the Blessed Sacrament in majestic meter, "*Fracto demum Sacramento, ne vacilles, sed memento tantum esse sub fragmento, quantum toto tegitur. Nulla rei fit scissura!*" But the poet's love inflames the dogma with a final blaze of wondering worship, as the cry of the lover follows quickly on the grave exposition, "*Ecce panis Angelorum, vere panis filiorum, non mittendus canibus!*" "Bread of children"—so indeed was the Eucharist to this royal scion of intellect who remained to the end of his life the simple child of God, one among those by whom the greatest Teacher of all times declared the kingdom of heaven to be tenanted and possessed. So, too, the life of Thomas Aquinas drew to its close.

The doctrine of the angel of the schools grew increasingly brilliant as his soul came to enjoy an ever-deepening union with God. On his very deathbed, this superb thinker expounded the Canticle of Canticles to the monks kneeling around him. Here was the dying Thomas, still master of the intellectual world of his time. But then the Blessed Sacrament was brought to him. And, with a supreme and well-nigh incredible effort, the man so huge in body, so gigantic in mind, managed to rise from his deathbed and prostrate himself before the Sacred Host. Here was the undying Thomas, child and disciple of the Divine Master, humble lover of the sacramental Jesus.

It is a superb tableau to imprint on our minds, to press against our own hearts: the humble Christ, hidden beneath the simple sign of bread; the mastermind of Christendom prostrate like a fallen warrior before his King. And it is a truer likeness of the saint than any artist's portrait that has come down to us. Thomas of Aquin—thinker, poet, doctor, lover,—a huddled bulk of humble worship before his sacramental God. Thomas indeed found all delight, all knowledge, all strength in the Blessed Sacrament. With him, to say, *"Omne delectamentum in se habentem,"* was to give a simple statement of his own soul, the single-phrase dissertation on his own spiritual life. "Down in adoration falling, lo! the sacred Host we hail!" Never a Benediction service, but those burning words of the Angelic Doctor are sung. And we see him living his poetry, demonstrating his theses, as he flung his massive, weakened body from the couch of death to fall down in adoration before his Eucharistic God.

The stricken warrior received his Divine Master for the last time, and his limpid soul seemed to find a tongue of its own to give vigor to the faltering speech of the dying. The great voice rang out as in the days when it had thrilled the intelligentsia of Paris, Bologna, and Rome. "I receive you," cried the prince of theologians, "the price of the redemption of my soul, for whom I have studied, watched, preached and taught." Here was the epitome of all his teaching, the fine apex of all his discourses.

We pray the oration of the Blessed Sacrament how many hundreds and hundreds of times in our religious lives, asking always that "we may perceive within ourselves the fruit of redemption." And we also pray a qualifying phrase: that by venerating the sacred mysteries of Christ's Body and Blood this fruit of redemption may appear. When, like St. Thomas, we can fall down before our Eucharistic Lord and honestly affirm that it is for Him alone, for Him so humbly hidden on our altars, for Him so wounded by, and patient with, the apathy of His own, for Him that we have studied and watched, preached and taught, then we, too, shall perceive within ourselves the fruit of redemption. We shall know with the joyous conviction of the master thinker of all times and the poet laureate of the Blessed Sacrament, that here is all delight. And our religious lives will catch the coruscations of that same Incarnate, Transubstantiated Love that set the heart of St. Thomas on fire—*Omne, omne delectamentum in se habentem*. For Thomas has more to teach us than the contents of his theses and defenses. He has sounded the mysteries of the silence and the song.

XI

CHESTERTON AND THE FRANCISCAN HEART

ALMOST THIRTY YEARS HAVE ELAPSED since the death of England's greatest literary giant of modern times. The dissenting voices to that claim are so relatively feeble as to be drowned past hope of literary tugboats in the universal roar of acclaim that continues to thunder the name of the bulky genius whose voluminous opera cape ("worn mostly for concealment, my dear!") no longer eddies down Fleet Street or flaps on Notting Hill. The lovable prince of paradox has been plaudited by the pens of the litterateurs less great only than himself, and the knight of lost causes has been crowned with laurel by every heart that holds a spark of the poetry that flamed in his own.

What is there left to say?

To any who has felt his pulse quicken to the cannonaded best of "Lepanto," to any whose heart has leaped up to the challenge of *Manalive*, to any who has romped with the *Greybeards at Play* and joined that extravagant chorus, that is a begging question!

And to any Franciscan heart that has quickened to the near-divine tunes of this twentieth century's pied piper of Charing Cross, it will not suffice that every other tongue under heaven has sung the piper's praises. There must still be a Franciscan word for him. Now, on no two souls (or so it seems to me), can the genius of Chesterton strike the same chord. To those who live, as distinct from those who exist, a charge is made on every mood and shade of their being by this man who is at will the lightest and laughingest rimester, the profoundest theologian, the most speculative of philosophers, the most delicately fanciful of poets. He has plumbed the deeps of metaphysical thought, until Etienne Gilson, that most distinguished Thomistic scholar, could quietly avow that Chesterton's work on Saint Thomas is the "best book written on the subject." He has breathed in the rarefied air of mystical theology; the unfortunate Father Leonard Feeney was in good theological repute when he declared that, by his finding, Chesterton had never written a line contrary to Catholic doctrine, nor a word that could come under theological suspicion. He has quaffed the most ancient wines of poetry, and written some of the most poignantly lovely lines in modern poetry. Where could we find a lovelier song for our Lady than this delicate lyric:

> "... rising from play at your pale raiment's hems,
> God, grown adventurous from all time's repose,
> Of your tall body climbed the ivory tower
> And kissed upon your mouth the mystic rose."

Chesterton and the Franciscan Heart

Gilbert Keith Chesterton introduced me to St. Francis. He prepared me beforehand to meet my future Father (an odd relationship peculiar to religious!) when, at thirteen, I found an intriguing title wedged in among the lines of those more prosaic appellations indigenous to high school library shelves: *The Poet and the Lunatics*. I was enthralled!

It having been my delight for some years past to spend my summers reading poetry (and—whisper it!—writing what only a fond mother could call by that same name), and such pursuits being considered a mild form of lunacy by my roller-skating contemporaries, I thought I had found my book. Actually, I had found more than I knew. The poet Gabriel Gale was really the mirror of Chesterton himself. And Chesterton, a generous mirror of Saint Francis.

Gabriel Gale stood on his head because the world was upside down. Saint Francis stood thirteenth-century society on its head until whole regiments in it saw with a shock of complete wonderment that their world really *was* upside down, that it spent its whole energy tracking down treasures that provided convenient sustenance for moths and offered ready metal for the tongues of rust. Gabriel Gale, who would endeavor to appear transparent if an agonizing psychopath avowed the world was made of glass, was impelled by the same impetus that flung the arms of the Poverello around spiritual as well as physical lepers, and made him the friend of any and every creature bearing the divine copyright.

As I read of the "liberalist" who began by inveighing against the slavery of faith, progressed to dashing chairs to pieces because their legs formed crosses, and ended with blowing up houses because they had walls, I was reading, too, of the "reformers" of Francis' day who, while the Little Poor Man was quite literally reforming society to its first Christian cast, were themselves reforming nothing, but only forming new and ghastly miasmas from the swamps of their heresies.

I learned, as I went on sharing this alarmingly literal Christian's simple joy in the wonders of God's creation, what it means to be a man alive. You will recall that the remarkable thing about Innocent Smith, the engaging hero of G.K.'s *Manalive,* was that the fellow was invariably and under the most trying circumstances, a man alive. So was Chesterton—a man alive to the supernatural overtones of every encounter in life, thrilling to all the tremendous trifles that preface the book of eternity, clinging, like his monk in *The Ball and the Cross,* to the Cross, and viewing all things in its perspective. He knew, as Francis knew, that a left-hand hold on the Cross with the right hand closed tightly on the purse, is a precarious posture and one that will not long defy the law of divine gravity. A purse can hold many false coins other than common currency: license, mediocrity, bigotry, and self-complacency, to mention only a few. Whatever it contains, it needs a tight hand; and, as Chesterton and St. Francis knew so well, one gets no secure hold on God with one hand only. He is a loving God, wanting a full-armed embrace, not a polite and cautious salute.

Both men knew these things; both men realized that the world needed something extraordinary in the line of jolts if it were to grasp the same truths.

So they set about becoming two of the most original men society has known by being the most unoriginal. G.K. Chesterton was only what Papini has urged every Christian to be: a plagiarist of Christ. And Francis Bernardone was merely an imitator, so thoroughgoing an imitator that the people of his age gave him a title that has come down through seven centuries to move our lesser hearts to a love so grateful that it is never far from tears. They called him, "The Christ of Umbria."

Chesterton and the Franciscan Heart

The title, "prince of paradox," sits well on Chesterton who knew so well that jaded sympathies and near-sighted souls must have truth turned inside-out and round-about before they are excited to a response. He used paradox as a constant medium to help us realize truth for what it is: the vast unchangeable. But Someone knew this before him; Someone else was truly the Prince of paradox.

Christ cautioned: "Unless you be converted and become as little children..." (Mt 18:3). The converted Chesterton, in the gorgeous *Greybeards at Play*, calls a child, "the sage of whom I learn." Christ demanded no erudition of His followers, only that they "... learn of Me, because I am meek and humble of Heart" (Mt 11:29). Chesterton wrote regretfully of *The Man Who Knew Too Much*. Christ insisted: "Unless you eat the Flesh of the Son of Man and drink His Blood..." (Jn 6:54). Chesterton spoke lovingly of the "little window where God sits all the year," and, "whence the world looks small and very dear." So indeed did the world, however shabby it looked to the rest of men, look to Chesterton: dear, because it was modeled by God's hands and sanctified by the footsteps of His Son; small, because this man had the happy faculty of viewing all things in the light of the large and eternal truths.

In the same way, St. Francis sang for sheer joy because he had nothing under the sun, but only a Father above it. He prophesied that his talisman, *"Pax et bonum!"* would one day be uttered as far as the girdle of earth reaches, because he knew that peacemakers are the children of God! He promised riches past counting to those who threw away the small change of earth. He despatched troops of barefoot friars with neither scrip nor staff. Nothing he did was original. He only copied his divine Master.

But he gave mediocrity the nastiest jolt it had received since the lifetime of the Christ. And God Himself sealed his approval on this absolute Christian. He signed Francis with the royal insignia of His Son, the sacred stigmata, as though He Himself wished the resemblance to be as entire as Omnipotence could make it.

Against two such Christians as St. Francis and Chesterton, the world had to muster some defenses. So it called St. Francis an impractical fool; Chesterton, a mere juggler of words. It dared not deny the charm and lovableness of both. The men and women who, each year, continue to rush into the arms of the Franciscan family and beg to be numbered among its members are sufficient comment on the impracticability of the Franciscan ideal. And, if it is true that one easily falls spellbound under the phraseology of Chesterton, it is only necessary to go back and look beneath the words to find the truth he has objectified in magic. Remembering the giant's counsel to the child in *Greybeards at Play*, I wonder whether this is not the secret alike of paradox and sanctity. Chesterton wrote:

> I looked at him, and only said:
> 'Go on! the world is round!'

Is not that paradox?—truth gone all around the world to meet itself and find itself the same! Is not that the only possibility of genuine sanctity—that roundness of prayer and of action, which springs from the Christ and returns there!

Who could delineate the character of Chesterton? Certainly not I. His is a sprawling genius, defying compactness. And who will say that his is the final word on St. Francis? One is very safe in prophesying that 1985 will find the world library on St. Francis the richer by five new books on the Little Poor Man. I rather think Chesterton himself gave us the satisfactory description of himself and his mission when he wrote of the saint he so ardently loved and for whose ideals his own great physical, mental, and spiritual bulk provided a perfect sounding board. Chesterton declared that

Chesterton and the Franciscan Heart

St. Francis was, "an extraordinary man sent to encourage ordinary men to be ordinary with an extraordinary exultation."

So was Chesterton.

XII

SIMPLICITY

THE TRAGIC DEATH of that authentic lyricist, Dylan Thomas fanned smoldering poetic controversies on the connotative value of words into a discursive blaze. Unlike many such conflagrations, this one was worth the scorch of an audition. For, it is astonishing how much of atmosphere a word can evoke, what tortured connotations an innocent term can be victimized into bearing. Quite aside from the individualized and specialized connotative value and extra definitive meaning of words (of which there are as many examples, perhaps, as there are persons) is that general overtone a term comes in time to strike on all ears, that shifting etymological twilight in which a particular word can so lose its form as to become a kind of nebulous contradiction of itself. Such a word is: simplicity.

Simplicity

Perhaps the most misused of spiritual terms, simplicity has suffered a martyrdom of falsification. A popular recording of the tender classic, "*Le Jongleur de Notre Dame*," snaps one out of a hushed appreciation of high drama with the tone of its quite remarkable final statement. "Blessed," solemnly whispers the abbot upon beholding the miracle, "are the simple of heart; for they also shall see God." One is made to feel that simplicity may yet manage to push into some corner of Paradise not occupied by the scintillating complexity of the gifted. "They *also*..." Even the simple. There is no mistaking the inflection on the record. We are given to feel that we the wise, we the complex, can afford to be indulgent on occasion and make room for the simple.

Who are the simple? Those who talk of "simple souls" after the manner of persons patting a dull child on the head, may be embarrassed to be reminded that God is simple, that He is, in fact, Simplicity. One marvels at the alchemies of tongue and mind, whereby the Name of God has come to connote for men those of the largo intelligence and the life circumscribed by futility. The mentally nondescript, the stolid souled, those incapable of exquisite suffering or the high adventure of the spiritual life, are herded together with patronizing prods, labelled "simple souls," and left to graze, while we turn to persons more interesting. Yet, the thunder of the voice of God remains. "I Am Who Am." Pure Being. Oneness. Simplicity.

It may be that the most potent factor in inclining us to so false, even so absurd, a concept of simplicity is a subconscious fear of recognizing simplicity for what it truly is, and the consequent demands on ourselves. Perhaps in that inner court of our heart where the memory of our paradisal infancy in the universal womb of Eve keeps the strain of ruined songs, we will admit to a deeper understanding of simplicity than we care to admit by our actions.

We could juxtapose Pope's familiar words about vice into a telling comment on simplicity:

> Simplicity seems a dodderer of so nondescript a mien
> As to be scorned, needs only to be seen;
> But seen too oft, familiar with her face,
> We may begin to quail, then wonder, then embrace.

To be simple is to be, in as full a sense as a child of fallen parents can hope to be, a person restored to his integrity. The simple man is a man of one purpose who travels a straight road home to his God. He is a man who knows why he was created, where he is going, and how to get there. His eyes are fixed on a single point, on a peak so majestic that the falls and wounds and heartscalds which are inevitable companions of the journey, seem negligible to him. There is quite a sound analogy of the simple soul in the person of the ardent mountainclimber. To the great bulk of us valley-dwellers, there is something foolhardy about these shining-eyed fools who risk life and limb for the joy of cresting a tall hill. We read of them, weary and torn, strapped and swinging, dangling and tumbling; and we feel quite superior with our reasonable knitting and our detective thriller. It may be that the climbers think, in the alpine silences of their own hearts, that they are far more practical-minded than some others. They have a purpose.

The analogy may have a point to score, but it limps beside the spiritual splendor of the virtue. We grasp truth best by the living example. And if we want a perfect example of what simplicity truly and exquisitely is, then we need look only to the person of the Little Poor Man, that engaging fool of the Lord whom society has ever deplored as a madman, and the members of society continued to love with an astonishing tenderness: St. Francis of Assisi.

Simplicity

Francis had a fairly good start down the winding paths of complexity when he thought it reasonable to be two persons at once: the roisterer and the soul of prayer. It is comforting to know that the Poverello (though for a considerably shorter period than most of us) thought it highly possible and certainly pleasurable to have one's cake and eat it, too. If Holy Church describes us as "poor, banished children of Eve," sentenced to "exile in a valley of tears," the young Francis felt decidedly rich and highly unbanished. If earth was a place of exile, it was a very jolly island. He could not hear the tear-splash for the laughter.

Then came his "conversion." The term is a favorite with the saints who use it in its pristine beauty of meaning, not with the sorry memories it may evoke for the rest of us. Francis' conversion was indeed a turning about. We think of a conversion as a turning from vice, error, and their unhappy company. We seldom run the word or the event down to its etymological lair. Willing to turn from the things that offend God, we can still fail to turn about with Him to the things that are His. That is where we part company with St. Francis who wholly turned about to the vision given once to every man to see, and who thus became the simplest of souls.

Equivocation became an impossibility for him after that. Complexity ran out of the pores of his soul like the saving sweat after fever, and left him a man of such perfect spiritual vision and such utter integrity that it did not strike him as poignant (though it assuredly strikes us so) that, physically nearly blind at the end of his life, unable to bear the light of the sun on his tortured eyes, he should sing of "little brother sun" with affection and admiration. To such a soul whose gaze was fastened on a certain goal and whose feet were set on a straight path, it was no hardship of spirit to take God at His word. If Christ had said thus and so in the

Gospel, Francis would do thus and so. This was all too simple for the complexity of the thirteenth century. It is far too simple for us. And so a lack of spiritual integrity in some who love Francis of Assisi shields its eyes against the awful simplicity of the saint by picturing him as merely a very good natured and lovable fellow who patted rabbits on the head and inaugurated the bird-watchers' society, and who was exceptionally generous to the poor.

To consider how generous Francis was to *God* brings us to such matters as the broken-bodied and brokenhearted man weeping over the apparent ruin of his order and his dreams, to the riven hands and feet of the stigmatized lover whom Holy Church calls "the seraphic St. Francis," to the saint who was so simple, so at one with himself and his God that all nature was but the thinnest of veils thrown over the Face of God.

The man who has shed his inner complexity is at once rewarded with purified vision. The edge of his thought processes is sharpened, so that his insight cuts like a powerful scythe through the tangle of materialities. He does not so much strive to acquire and to preserve a right sense of values; he is already in possession of it by inheritance. However ruined our paradise, we keep our pathetic heirship. And it is only by attaining to simplicity that we come of age to claim our legacy of vision.

Through the red haze of pain that marked his inglorious exit from Eden, Adam beheld one sharp swordpoint of light. With senses darkened and bestial instincts awakened, with the drums of our endless war with ourselves beginning their bizarre music in his heart, Adam had the knowledge gained by the first of mankind's centuried train of falls. Now he knew. Knew with every bead of strange, new sweat, with every unaccustomed ache of muscle, with every gagging loneliness stopping his throat with pain,—all he had lost. And he understood with a new and exquisitely painful humility that things would not always be so. He had an incredible, glorious promise in the very core of the curse he must bear. One day a Woman would exonerate his own weeping Eve. One far morning, a Son of his would spring the lock of heaven in his favor. Adam must certainly have been a simple man. No one ever knew with greater poignancy what mattered and what did not.

We are decades of centuries further from paradise, and simplicity comes harder to us. The taste of a lost perfection does not tantalize our spiritual hunger as it did Adam's. Yet, there is not one heartscald of loss nor one bruise of misunderstanding that does not testify to where our ancestral home is and how far we have wandered away from it. It is significant that complex souls chafe endlessly under the burden of reality, whereas the simple accept the grim reality of their heritage with the same spiritual calm with which they enjoy the painful bliss of the promise.

Simple souls are not at all the phlegmatic "smilers" they are often depicted to be. They are souls of burning tears and mighty laughter. They can wander through nights of pain with St. Francis, weeping with him because "Love is not loved." And they can match him step for skip and joy for song when Francis fashions himself a "fiddle" of two sticks to make merry music because God is his Father and heaven is his home. It may seem a paradox in itself to maintain that only the simple can grasp the seeming complexity of a paradox. But the really complex soul lacks the clarity of vision to see that paradox is only truth standing upon its head or traveled around the universe to shake its own hand.

To accept humbly and simply the fact that earth is a vale of tears, designedly so since the primal human sin, is to hold the key to all the mysteries of pain and loss and sorrow. To know that, after this, our exile, the Mother of God will answer the repeated cry of Holy Church and of every Christian heart and will indeed

Simplicity

"show us the blessed Fruit of her womb," is to be a man half wild with joy. And to realize we are not citizens of the world, but exiles in the world, is the explanation for everything that would otherwise clutter and cloud our lives. It is a realization that only simple men are equipped to grasp. Men like St. Francis of Assisi.

XIII

THE SINGLE TRAGEDY

L IVING IN THE MIDST of fist-swinging and heartwringing racial crises at home, and new governments not so much forming as erupting abroad, while our communist cousins hold out friendship bouquets with hydrogen bombs in their back pockets, and while our own personal stack of frustrations mounts as we try to catch the coattails of our jet-speed days long enough to discover what is happening to the world and to us, and why, we might seem equipped to draw up an imposing number of present or prospective tragedies. Yet, the real fact is that the magnificent declaration of the eminent French writer, Leon Bloy, remains as true as when he uttered it. And he uttered it toward the close of a life which would certainly qualify as tragic in most persons' reckoning. He said, "There is only one tragedy, not to be one of the saints."

Spaces for Silence

The notion falls with an alien clang on our modern mentality. Many persons are a little embarrassed at the idea. We can limit our horizons so consistently with materialities, shrink our souls so miserably with mediocrity and compromise, that the concept of personal heroic sanctity seems preposterous. But Bloy's words could well be blazoned across the lintel of the universe, and in the Blood of the King of all saints: "There is only one tragedy, only one failure—not to have been one of the saints." To remember that is to keep all human affairs in correct perspective. A man called to be a saint cannot be contented with being part of a mass, even in an age where it is easy to lose the sense of personal destiny, with every woman apparently ambitious to look like every other woman, and every man aspiring to be part of the organization.

We can gradually back out of our own lives and sit on the sidelines of our own destiny. Our newspapers think for us, our television sets enslave us; some of our education has turned into a mere induction of facts, so that graduates are turned out as warehouses of accumulated information, rather than as individuals trained to culture the soil of their intellect. But it is our appointed Christian task to cling to faith in a personal destiny. To be loved by the Creator of heaven and earth: this is each man's dignity. To be destined by God for sanctity: this is each man's nobility.

Ours is an age of mass production and wholesale drive, when it is almost natural to measure humanity, like machinery, in bulk. In the era of the individual craftsman, personal dignity needed no such defense as it needs today. It was taken for granted. However, if a sense of high personal destiny was more palpable yesterday, it is no less real today. That the Son of God would have given himself to be crucified for a single human soul is a truth of such proportions that we prefer merely to admit it rather than to ponder it. We who measure by size, glory in faceless bulk, pride ourselves on quickness and quantity, are startled by such a God.

This God of ours Who dwells in light inaccessible is often closest to human intellect by paradox. We need truth shaken up and turned inside out. So it is with the concept of a personal destiny to sainthood. Paradox will tell it best. It is only the man intensely conscious of his singularity, the unique quality of *his* creation and destiny, who can be a truly socially conscious person. Not the "rugged individual" of the popular novel who is only a *poseur*, an isolationist in the glittering hermitage of his egoism. No, but the man profoundly aware of his individual dignity.

To weatherproof our lives with a pietousness which is impervious to social injustice on our own block or in our own community center, to the basic human needs of those whose lives brush ours not by happenstance but by divine maneuver, is to fail in respect and love for others because we have first failed in respect and love for ourselves. We do not betray other human beings unless we have first betrayed ourselves. Obviously, if we do not live in the consciousness of a personal destiny to sainthood which demands of us not something but everything, we are not going to be aroused by the personal destiny of others nor shall we be interested in helping them fulfil it.

Papini has said that every Christian should be a plagiarist of Christ. Now Christ has declared that those who lose their lives, shall save them. We can plagiarize His divine paradox and declare that to be profoundly conscious of one's personal destiny is to lose oneself in the most socially significant of acts. To come to the most intense awareness of one's personal destiny and to fulfil it, is to become a saint. It requires only earnest love and a true grasp of the staggering greatness to which we are called, to be saints.

Christ went further than the first command to "love your

neighbor as yourself" when on the very threshold of His death agony, He asked that we love others as He has loved us. What does this mean? A vaguely benevolent feeling toward Humanity, Inc.? A membership card in the local unit of Brotherhood International? For Christ, it entailed being misused and put upon, it meant weariness and exhaustion, it was a matter of service repaid usually with ingratitude and sometimes with hypocrisy and betrayal. And He went on loving the unheeding, the graceless, the mocking and scheming unlovables among men. In the end, He died for them. This is the kind of greatness to which we are called. And it *is* staggering, too staggering for those who want a more prophylactic piety than the sweating commitment of one's whole being to the radical demands of Christianity. Yet, such a commitment can be made in the kitchen. It is a workable thesis in the office.

A destiny to sainthood cannot fail to impose a burden of sacrifice and suffering, but the burden of God is lighter than the miseries of mediocrity. The yoke of Divinity is infinitely sweeter than the fetters of self-gratification and pleasure-seeking. By the fine irony of God, we suffer far more in our attempts to evade suffering than do the saints who embrace suffering for Love's sake. It is all so very simple that our minds, too accustomed to artificial complexities, cannot quite grasp such a lucid principle. As Chesterton said: "The way is all so very plain that we may lose the way. . . so very simple is the road, that we may stray from it."

Our generation has the dubious distinction of numbering more cases of mental collapse than any preceding one. Perhaps it is the misdirection of the soul's energies that account for it. When a man pledges himself to the world, employs his whole strength to avoid that suffering which is the very birthright of our fallen race, he is guilty of a spiritual perversion, and his immortal soul takes its revenge. The very nobility of his intellect turns against him. Our wild flight from suffering may be our undoing as a nation as well as our eternal personal loss. Our switches and gadgets and cushions multiply. Sometimes multiple sclerosis of the soul sets in along with them. There is a great deal of truth in Dorothy Thompson's observation that souls made impervious to, even schooled against, a true personal dignity as being the real social significance, turn to despair. The saint, vibrantly aware of his glorious personal destiny, his divine heredity, is quickened to all beauty and thus can retain his innate intuition of the intangibles even in the midst of external squalor and meanness. The saint can never despair. The saint is always an optimist. Could one believe in a personal destiny of sanctity, a divine sonship, a heavenly heritage, and be a pessimist?

Not to believe in one's own destiny of sainthood is to live a drab and meaningless life, and to be unequipped to cope with suffering when it inevitably arrives. On the other hand, to believe in it is consciously to accept the integrity of all creation, the economy of suffering, the purposiveness of circumstance and situation. And this is to realize the eschatological significance of all that we do. It is to enter into the joy of St. Paul when he cries out: "We have not here a lasting city" (Heb 13:14). That statement is not a mental hot-water bottle. It is the triumphant outcry of a man with a purpose in life, a purpose in eternity.

Our destiny is bliss. Our home is heaven. To remember that is to transfigure the most drab life into a blaze of beauty, to transmute the brass of daily sorrows into the pure gold of hope, to transform the mean shape of earthly circumstances into the contours of glory. Our Lord told a mystic of our times: "Love souls for what they are capable of becoming." Let us love ourselves, too, for what we are capable of becoming, even in the next moment. Such love is the Christian self-respect, the love in the mind of Christ Who counseled us to love others "as ourselves." And what are we not capable of becoming, who are capable of becoming saints?

St. Francis of Assisi had a particular talent for striking gold in the most unpromising human soil. He never hesitated to encourage robbers to be saints, misers to be Christian spendthrifts, sensual men to become ascetics. No one had a stronger sense of other men's destiny to sanctity because no one was more happily driven by the sense of his own. Francis could never lower himself enough because he understood that God desired to lift him up. And his whole life was truly a divine comedy with a very happy ending. For him, manifestly, there was not that single tragedy—not to have been one of the saints.

XIV

CLARE OF ASSISI: SAINT FOR NOW

MANY PERSONS HAVE BEEN ARRESTED by the new perspective on hagiography given in the popular, *Saints for Now*. The fact that none of the gifted authors in the galaxy of literary talent represented there thought that Clare of Assisi was a saint-for-now may be a tribute to the obscurity she fostered, but it is also a judgment on our purblind age. And this, though the charming compiler of the studies bears her name! The saints whose lives are sketched in the engaging collection can all ably prove their claim to belong to our "now," but their company would certainly have been enriched by a certain barefoot nun with little laughter wrinkles around her beautiful, illness-hollowed eyes, and lips shaped as well for singing as for compassion. Two of the literateurs chose our seraphic Father Saint Francis as the saint-for-now. Did no one think of the utterly lovely lady whose life was the incarnation of his ideals?

Spaces for Silence

To recognize Clare of Assisi as a saint-for-now, we need first to clarify the needs and to study the complexion of our times. Who was it said, so deliciously, that the hero of whom he wrote was "born in a troubled age—just as everyone else is!" It is easy to subscribe to the dour philosopher's view, crediting our age as the most desperately wicked of all epochs. Perhaps it is. We have managed to systematize cruelty rather beyond anything our forbears did in that line. We have commercialized sin and made it a paying enterprise. We have also, however, proved that our wells of charity and goodness are far from dry, and have manifested a compassion far more vast than its antithetical cruelty. Our age is probably no more diabolically evil than the age which ignited Christians' bodies for lamps in its Roman parks; probably no better than the age when craftsmen spent whole lives perfecting a turret of a cathedral, or kings marched to the Crusades. But it has its particular deficiencies, the first of which seems to be a lack of thoroughgoing courage. This is particularly evident in our own country where the vast majority are content to compromise with evil rather than to fight a clear-cut battle for the truth they own and the ideals they profess. Compromise is often a sin against courage, and we have become adept in its practice. Compromise and expediency are the watchwords taken up to silence the small clamor of consciences. And we like to forget that it is supernatural prudence which is praiseworthy, and that the prudence of men often gives insult to God.

Clare of Assisi was incapable of compromise where there was no room for alternative. We can all dream over the romance of her elopement to Saint Mary of the Angels, her investiture in the rough robe of poverty, her adamant stand against all and whomever opposed her ideals. Can we likewise rouse ourselves to a vital concept of what courage a girl of eighteen, wealthy, lovely, cherished, and pursued, required to become the first daughter of the Poverello? Francis was an enigma to those to whom he was not an object of suspicion. His little ragged band of friars had no official status in the Church at that time. He had no security to offer the beautiful young Clare, not even to the extent of the next day's dinner (and one wonders where he contrived to get the shabby habit he threw over her satin gown!)—nothing, in effect, but a dream as mad as the Gospel and his personal guarantee that, as his daughter, she would always be entitled to nothing at all.

Clare was no more a "dreamer" in the modern accepted sense of that word than was Francis. Chesterton has said that most of us are so "off-center" in our mediocrity that we juxtapose our position with that of the true "centrics" and arrive at the remarkable conclusion that the truesighted genius and the literal-minded saint are the eccentrics. Our Father St. Francis and our Mother St. Clare were so centric that the world could defend its own pathetic dullness and cowardice only by calling them "eccentric dreamers." Such courage as Clare had, to stake absolutely everything on a principle she knew to be sound and true, is the antidote for our age poisoned with pusillanimity and the small, crawling fears for our comfort, our false security, our cultivated lethargy. The courage of a young girl who thought true values worth the highest stakes is the draught of fresh air needed in our hothouse world of today. And, if we tend to dwell only on the beauty of the act of humiliation when Clare gripped hold of the altar with one hand and snatched off her veil with the other to uncover her shorn head before her raging relatives, we might also find there a trace of Clare's delightful humor, the humor that true courage always begets. The shorn lamb of Francis, facing those fulminating Italians, says the equivalent of: "And that, my dears, is that!" If we have forgotten how to laugh, it is because we have lost courage.

Spaces for Silence

Thirty years later, ill and worn, this same brave woman could issue calm orders above the hue and cry of the fast-approaching barbarian invaders, and then face them with the serenity of faith, while lifting up the Sacred Host for her single Defense and whispering to her Lover that sweet quasi-reproach of a sublime courage: "Deliver not, my Lord, to beasts, the souls of them who praise you." There never was a situation or a person to daunt Clare. When some of the first friars lost heart and courage for the ideal of their Father, Francis turned his sad steps to San Damiano where there was one heart that never knew any diminution of faith in him or courage to cling to his ideal. Meditating on the overwhelming griefs of our seraphic Father in those days of "too many friars" and too little courage, and on his humble turning to his first daughter for comfort and support, we feel a sense of warmest gratitude for Clare's constancy and the loyal courage of her Poor Ladies at San Damiano. The lines of Chesterton's exquisite carol might have been written as the cry of our Father Francis' anguished heart as it healed at the monastery of his daughters. "O weary, weary is the world, But here is all aright." Not even the Sovereign Pontiff could persuade her to turn a least left or a merest right from the straight path of her Father Francis' teaching. Again, there is a trace of Clare's quiet humor in her sweetly humble but calculatedly adamant reply to Pope Gregory IX: "Holy Father, absolve me from my sins, but not from my vow of poverty." Courage like Clare's could remake the face of our wavering society today.

With the cleanness of courage has gone the freshness of purity. Surely there is no need to defend the thesis that purity is a crying need of our polluted times. Our age has traded on lust so hard and so long, using it as the lure in advertisements, the cover-up for plotless, banal books, the theme of hit-parade songs, that Pope's classic lines are all too sturdily evidenced by our hard-faced young girls and our prematurely-old boys: "Sin is a monster of so horrible a mien, as to be hated, need only to be seen; but seen too oft, familiar with its face, we first endure, then pity, then embrace." Purity, above all other things, is the myrrh that preserves youth. And its conspicuous absence in our modern world explains why too many girls look like faded women. Without an affection for holy purity, the heart grows quickly old in the world's specious wisdom, and the body is listless before it has ever quickened to the vast universe of those joys visible only to the clean of heart.

The breviary has astonishing comments to make on St. Clare. The same childlike calm boastfulness of: "Our God is in heaven, and does whatever He pleases," asserts that Clare is "more shining than light." God created light as the first miraculous diffusion of His own splendor. Holy Church lets Clare's daughters claim that He made in their Mother something to outshine light itself. Each August 12[1], Poor Ladies throughout the world take up their breviaries and sing out, in how many hundreds of bare little choirs, that: "The brightness of Clare has filled the whole earth."

If we quote Chesterton again, let us lay the blame on his own surpassing love for St. Francis and St. Clare! It was GK who insisted that, "Chastity is not mere abstention. . . it is something (positive and) flaming." It was in Clare. Her purity was a white flame yearning up towards Love. It was radiant. It blazed. Only the pure really know how to love. And Clare, who was fashioned for loving, made no apologies for the rugged measures she took to preserve that wisdom. The thousands who endure tortures to effect a semblance of physical beauty in themselves shudder at the

---

[1] The feast of Saint Clare has been celebrated on August 12 until the 1970 Calendar revisions. It is currently celebrated on August 11.

notion of a perpetual fast, a continual silence, an endless cycle of vigils, and the other means Clare used to insure the beauty of her spirit and that of her daughters. With her, it was always a question of penance, yes—but penance for love's sake! She knew that without love, penance is as meaningless as turns on a trapeze. But she was not so foolish as to credit original sin in theory and not as a vital principle. The pure always fear for their purity. The impure do not trouble with precautions, having already slipped beyond them.

Belief in the Communion of Saints, the Mystical Body of Christ, was the second living principle actuating Clare in her life of penance. She knew that on the mysterious scales of Divine Justice, the penances of the Poor Ladies would avail for the impenitent in the world, that their purity would weigh against the impurity of others, that they would be accepted as victims for others' sins. Seven centuries before our Blessed Lady said to the children of Fatima: "Many souls go to hell because there is no one to pray and make sacrifices for them," Clare of Assisi was defending that thesis with her own and her daughters' lives of chastity and penance. A return to the humble paths of Clare who was "purer than light," could rekindle the blaze of youth in modern, hard, young faces, could release incredible vials of fragrance down the odorous streets of our stale age.

It is the nature of goodness to diffuse itself, and in quiet. It is the nature of evil to defend itself, and most often with noise. We have called Clare of Assisi the candle in Umbria, because that seemed the truest symbol of her life and of her soul. She who was brave against the dark as candleflame is brave, pure in her flicker of life as candlelight is pure, was also quiet in her sanctity as the constant candle is quiet in giving up all that makes it a candle. The real office of a candle is to cease to be a candle. And the basic business of one aspiring to perfection is to become Someone else. It is an extremely difficult business, for one does get so attached even to the unpleasant person one is! It has been said that the predominant evil of any age ultimately manages to scale cloister walls. If the world has found that a constant racket will, in time, fill in its thought chambers and outcry its conscience, religious need likewise to be careful that they do not camouflage a great lack of being with a great deal of doing. The hero of the hour is the man who can do the most things in the shortest possible time, but he makes a sorry monastic hero.

In her century, when abbesses were more often than not women-of-affairs, with huge temporal holdings and immense households, enjoying the prestige of worldly queens, Clare quietly shut herself up in dilapidated old San Damiano. And, at once, it was a monastery. Not because it was grand or picturesque or thriving, but because it was a house of prayer and a haven of silence where souls devoted themselves to the most intense of all activities: passivity. Most of the first Poor Ladies were noblewomen, one was a princess royal. To all of them, Clare offered nothing in substitute for the trumpeting and adulation they had known in the world, except prayer and solitude and poverty. She herself has left not even one colorful statement on the political character of her times. And if some popes have sought temporal counsel from certain saints, three popes sought at San Damiano the spiritual counsel of one whose only concern with the world was for its soul, a concern of quiet prayer and self-immolation. When the aged Innocent IV found himself prostrated by temporal tragedies as well as by spiritual anguish, he came to his "daughter and mother, the Lady Clare," not for a plan of action, but to renew his own soul in the quiet of her holiness. It has never been claimed that our holy Father St. Francis asked

Clare what to do about recalcitrants or schismatics; it is known that he found his own answers in her serene loyalty.

We learn nowhere so quickly and yet so profoundly as we learn in quiet. Because the world cannot bear to learn about itself or to look in on its own wizened soul, it fears and hates quiet. It hustles, because it cannot afford to think. It rivets and blares because it dare not be still. Ours is an age of accomplishment, but one draws in the breath to think of what real and lasting accomplishments could spring out of a return to the silence of contemplation. The very word, contemplation, ought to be the most companionable of words for any soul, since it is the term of our eternal destiny. Yet most persons are ill at ease with it. Action and noise are less demanding companions. By modern standards, Clare of Assisi's life was wasted. She built no hospitals, introduced no system of pedagogy, made no speeches, wrote no books, did not even proclaim a new way of sanctity. The Gospel was her way. Francis was her guide. And her destiny was the quiet of utter union with God her Lover.

Clare had a taste for solitude and a talent for quiet. By indulging the one and perfecting the other, she learned the secrets of the King, and gained open sesame to His Heart. Her first spiritual daughters have told us of their Mother's increasing hunger for hours of companionship with her Divine Spouse in the quiet of private prayer. The Poor Clares' prayer schedule would probably seem staggering to most persons. For St. Clare, it was never sufficient. When her daughters slept, Clare remained before the Blessed Sacrament, lost in the quiet of her perfect union with God. How many times her daughters saw flames or rings of light about her head when she knelt in quiet prayer, oblivious of earth! Her quiet, "useless" life brought her to such intimacy with Christ that when dying she could say to Him with a sweet simplicity, "I thank You for having created me." Hers was the true courtesy of her seraphic Father. One is reminded of Mother Janet Stuart of our own times who died, not with a protest of *her* love for God on her lips, but with a Franciscan cry of simple wonder: "Oh, how He loves me!" In the simple song that was Clare's life, the ictus was always on God!

Clare is the saint of silence. If our holy Father St. Francis resembled our Lord as no other saint quite did, who will gainsay our belief that St. Clare most resembled the Holy Mother of God? She has left us no autobiography, no guidebooks, no "accomplishments." Just as our Blessed Lady did, she has left us the legacy of her quiet. We need it so acutely, we poor, noisy, busy little people, that we could well cry out like thunder: Clare is the saint-for-now! Her courage, her blazing purity, her perfect quiet are her claims to twentieth-century veneration. Her valor sweetly rebukes our pusillanimity; her exquisite purity pleads for our stale generation; the great, missionary heart that beat for all the world in the silence of her cloister, sends its throb across seven centuries to us now. If we look for light in these dark days, let us hear our seraphic Father's simple directive, uttered over and over again to sufferers of his own age and confided to our age from Heaven: "Go to the Lady Clare."

XV

CLARE OF ASSISI: WOMAN OF FAITH

I F THERE ARE FALSE CONNOTATIONS of words, there are also false connotations of saints. Sometimes Clare of Assisi is betrayed by both. For she was an idealist and a saint; or, more precisely, she was in a preeminent degree what every saint must be: an idealist.

What does that word too often connote in popular speech? Is it not the impractical dreamer, the poet sitting with chin propped on his fist and sighing at the harsh realities of life even while he longs to escape into a shadow-world of perfection? How often the phrase, "poets and dreamers," is tossed about with a kind of supercilious if indulgent pity for those who cannot face the rawness and roughness of actual life and so withdraw into unreality. A dreamer is presumed by some to be one who will not admit that life frequently involves nightmares of the soul and heart and mind. An idealist is supposedly a refugee from reality. And while they admit that dreams and ideals are tolerable and even salutary for the young, and should not be wholly abandoned by adults, practical men of affairs know that dreams and ideals will obviously require considerable adjustments for those of middle years.

In the end, what such people mean by an "idealist" who persevered as such into mature years, is someone who did not make the prescribed adjustments, that is, compromises. Clare of Assisi would qualify for them as one of that species. And her cloistered life would probably be summed up something like this: caught up into the first romantic glamor of the Franciscan movement, she rushed from her castle home, shut herself up in a poor monastery where harsh realities could not reach her, and sighed her way to heaven!

Truth to tell, Clare was not the popular false connotation of an idealist, but an idealist in the true meaning of the word: she was a woman who regarded reality as essentially spiritual. How superficial all this talk of the mutual exclusiveness of idealism and realism is. Who is actually equipped to cope with hard reality *except* the idealist? Once the shining ideal is obscured, the pressure of the teeming realities of life becomes coercive. Reality unillumined by the idealism that hopes against hope and believes in the humanly impossible can only lead to frustration. In the end, only the idealist can survive reality, the kind of idealist Clare was.

If the connotation of Clare for some is that of remoteness from reality, the true meaning of Clare is faith, that supreme faith which is the glory of a woman. It is faith alone which gives strength to deal with present realities. And this is where woman is endowed by nature above man, as man is endowed by nature above her in speculative reasoning.

Grace builds on nature, and it is the nature of woman to have faith: faith in man who has been set above her and whose helpmate she was created to be, faith in God, Who made her so to be. Any normal woman knows that a certain kind of subjection is her glory.

If we wish to determine the spiritual stature of a man, we can look to see what kind of woman loves him. Sometimes it is only the faith of the woman who loves that discovers and later sustains the greatness of the man. Far from relinquishing her natural womanly qualities, the woman consecrated to God actually rediscovers them on a higher spiritual plane. It is women who make practicable the ideals conceived by men, just as it is women who receive the great dreams of men into their own hearts and harbor them in faith through vicissitudes. Men go to war. Women wait. Men declare. Women affirm. Loyalty, which is stubbornness in faith, is one of God's superlative gifts to the nature of woman.

St. Francis of Assisi conceived the ideal which has come to bear his name, the Franciscan ideal. When it seemed in some degree to fail among men, it consistently and persistently succeeded among women. It sometimes wavered, but it worked at Clare's monastery of San Damiano. And when Francis himself seemed to waver, heartsick and weary with compromise and gloss, he went to Clare and rediscovered himself in her. For, this is what she always was: the mirror of Francis' first ideal, first faith, first dream.

It is all very romantic to think of wealthy young Clare dazzled by the novelty of Francis' preaching. Complete poverty and evangelical simplicity would have had the natural attraction of opposites for a high-minded girl whose life was steeped in luxuries and the complexities of a feudal society that was beginning to totter. The difference between Clare and many other young girls who might have felt the same attraction is that Clare had the faith to cling to her belief in the Franciscan ideal and make it a conviction.

Eloping, even into the cloister, has its romantic appeal, too. But it was, externally speaking, a rugged honeymoon Clare had. It is a different matter to theorize about the clutter of possessions than really to get clear of them. The rough robe Francis threw over her shoulders did not feel like the satin robes she had worn before, even though she had sometimes had a hairshirt under them. However much she prized it, it was hot. It scratched her fine skin. It weighed on her. And her hair! what an act of faith that was! Surely no man could completely understand this. Perhaps the shaggy-haired girls of today do not much understand it, either. But medieval Clare of the long golden ropes of waving hair, that sunlight of hair which was the glory of the Lombard women of Italy and her own outstanding natural possession.... There is no irreverence to God Who made the heart of a woman to accommodate His words to such a doffing of hair; in a sense, "greater love has no woman!" And we can be reasonably sure that St. Francis cut off that beautiful silk by the great fistfuls with quick and complete inexpertness.

What did young Clare of the cropped head and mean robe have to sustain her ideal? Faith. Absolutely nothing else. She had no convent, no community, no rule. She was quite a unique kind of foundress. But she had unlimited faith in the ideal of one small friar and his great dream. Never, from the shearing of her lovely hair until her last breath, did that faith waver.

Relatives pleaded and relatives stormed. Friends reasoned and reminded. But Clare was that kind of idealist who is not embarrassed by reality but who lifts reality out of the dust and informs it with the ideal. We need such idealism, we whose reality lies in a different dust—the dust of comfort and compromise.

When the beginning was made and the influx of subjects began, Clare's faith was tested and threatened on a new front. It is obvious that the legislator who sets down in her rule that contemptuous subjects shall take bread and water on the floor in the refectory for as many days as they continue obstinate, who reminds her daughters that worrying and fretting over the sins and faults of their companions only hinder charity in themselves and others, and who sternly cautions against envy, detraction, dissension, and division, had met some of humanity's more inglorious specimens. If she had set herself to live in a dream-world, she could never have so calmly legislated for the nightmares of religious life. Yet, she kept her faith in her daughters as she kept her faith in God.

There must occur for every idealist a period of crisis in which ideal and reality confront each other. The tragedy would be to agree to a peaceful coexistence by which would be meant that the ideal becomes escapism from the reality, a kind of twilight walk down which one wanders on brief excursions from the hard truth of things. How often Clare must have experienced what we often call by the misnomer of disillusionment, but which is actually only the labor pains of the ideal bringing forth its fruit, the ideal persisting in reality and fastening on the essential spirituality of things.

Clare knew how to be so gentle as to roam about the little monastery of San Damiano on cold pre-midnights to make sure her sleeping daughters were adequately blanketed. Yet, she had the sternness that could rebuke a nun she miraculously cured with some pointed reminders that if the nun did not change her line of conduct some worse ailment was likely to befall her. Here is the love of a woman strong in faith, loving the unlovable which we, too, must love and which we also often are.

Then there was the great trial, the very life-and-death struggle of her rule. Clare who so completely typified the Franciscan ideal had to live by a quasi-Benedictine rule for many years. She never fought against the authority that imposed it, but neither did she supinely accept it as ultimate. Rather, she persisted in faith. "I know in Whom I have believed!" (2 Tim 1:12) cried out St. Paul. St. Clare made that same wonderful act of faith. She knew. She believed. And so she lived on and suffered on, as women through the ages have known how to suffer and love and believe through wars and famines, through betrayals and desertions, through humiliations and defeats. God evidently prized Clare's faith very highly; for, He chose to reward it, which was really to end it, only two days before her death.

Clare was prostrate on her deathbed when Innocent IV sent her his *Solet Annuere,* the bull confirming her own rule. Absolute poverty was at last reinforced by the authority of Rome. The primitive Franciscan ideal was saved for the Second Order. Faith was crowned and triumphant. And so Clare died. She had fought the good fight of faith and had kept the faith. The course she finished was the course of lifelong faith. Therefore shall her daughters rise up and call her blessed!

XVI

Up Until This Time We Have Done Nothing

IF THE STATEMENT that not to advance in the spiritual life is to retreat, is a cliche, it nevertheless remains a truth. Movement is so essential to the religious vocation that where progression ceases, retrogression begins. It is an awesome consideration but one not without its own peculiar consolation. For, it is our poignant and paradoxical comfort to have the doors of nature's comfort shut against us. When we might desire to settle for a comfortable degree of holiness and nestle down into the rewarding warmth of our own regular observance, our own spiritual tidiness, our own convenient brand of "charity" which preserves continual serenity by the simple expedient of never rousing ourselves on any count!—we find this cozy chamber locked and bolted. No heart has ever yet found its own fulfilment short of eternity, but the religious vocation plants a seed of unrest more pregnant with power than the slimmer seed that is the common heritage of all men. Strangely, this unrest is our single genuine solace. Our inevitable failure ever to arrive at completion marks our dignity as the children of God, wandering in a land of exile but with the hope of returning one day to our fatherland.

What is this progression in the spiritual life? More precisely, what is it in the life of a Franciscan? Deprived of the odorous ease of stagnation, we should at least like to envision progress as a measured march from good to better to best unto heaven. The pious shops go on renewing their stock of those precious little pictures which show the religious, hair and draperies streaming, on the stairway to perfection. Invariably, our dear and long-suffering Lord is depicted as a trim-bearded figure in the background urging this languid lady to take another step, perhaps from humility to charity, or maybe another dainty advance from self-abnegation to patience. Each step is always neatly labelled. And we may safely infer that we shall become more delighted with ourselves on each new rise. Actually, nowhere is the piercing paradox of the spiritual life more stark and painful than in this consideration of spiritual progress.

We need not live long past our novitiate to begin squirming under the deepening instinct of what real progress is: the unfolding of our multifarious miseries, the revelation of our utter poverty of virtue, the acceptance of ourselves as wholly unlovable. We made a clean break with the persons and things we most cherished. We put on a poor habit and a common cord to testify we were the humble sons and daughters of the Poverello and wanted no part of earthly riches or greatness. We signed a solemn compact, with Holy Church for witness, giving over our rights to carnal love, proprietorship, and the direction of our own persons.

Surely these heroic folk who showed such unmistakable courage, who clung to such shining convictions against odds often heavy enough, who willingly gave the very core of their humanity into the open palm of the Divine Master, are persons to be trusted. They are men and women fitted to follow through to perfection such an auspicious beginning. What do we discover instead? The exact opposite.

Painfully, ashamedly, and then agonizingly we find ourselves out for tricksters and shamsters. We attain with little show of scholarship to the aching knowledge of our utter untrustworthiness. We discover the traitor in our own flesh and mind and spirit, the clever enemy who unravels all our resolutions and trips our stride at the very moment we had thought ourselves secure.

Here is the first interior crossroads. If our spiritual cheeks flame with embarrassment at discovering our essential meanness, then we shall never discover our essential greatness. We shall work so assiduously at discovering excuses for all our faults, at finding some others with whose conduct our own will compare excellently well, at taking refuge from the vision of our own failings in a pietous surprise at the sins and faults of others, that we shall throw our whole spiritual gaze out of focus. It takes heroic courage to face oneself for what one is. The alternative is self-deception, which throws a kind of mental tarpaulin over the field of spiritual combat in the soul, making it impervious alike to the sunlight of God's love and the rainfalls of His grace. On the other hand, if by strength of prayer and the superhuman effort which grace makes possible, we can force ourselves to accept ourselves for what we are, then we are immediately rewarded. Taking no step at all, we are set by God Himself on the first low rise of humility. The religious who does not realize himself to be capable of any sin and every fault has not even the first faint glimmer of humility. Conversely, the religious who has such a realization has indeed the preparation of soul necessary for the seed of humility, though *he* does not think so. It takes heroic courage to face oneself for what one is? Yes. But the reward is almost overpowering. It is peace, contentment, song.

Our Father St. Francis would never have needed a psychiatrist even had such services been as handy and accepted in his day as in ours. He never tortured his mind nor bedevilled his soul with the complex considerations of those who refuse to face the first and greatest of all natural realities—themselves. Surely no man ever suffered more poignantly over his own sins and the sins of the world than did the Little Poor Man. Surely no man had a more penetrating spiritual vision than he. Yet his conclusion was as calm as it was sound: "Lord, Who are You!—and who am I!"

It is small wonder that our seraphic Father could never seem to exhaust the meaning of the few words in that famous outcry of his. They express everything: our dignity and our ignobleness, our glory and our shame. They constitute a flaming protestation of love, and that particular kind of amazement which has always characterized Franciscans. They also betoken a humility whose profundity no other saint has plumbed more completely.

The Franciscan who refuses to face himself and call his faults by their true names, will make that cry of our holy Father a mere pious mouthing as far as he himself is concerned. We may address our Lord as, "Who are You!" and bow our heads with a, "Who am I!" and still be snowbound in our righteousness, secretly satisfied that we are not garrulous like Sister X nor hot-tempered like Father Y, and never guessing that our pride is far noisier than any chatter of tongues, and our complacency like foul water turned on the ardor of Love. "Never guessing" is indeed the final outpost in the desert of spiritual blindness concerning ourselves. We see this manifest all about us.

The young religious who cannot face herself builds up a leathery scar tissue on the wounds of correction and reproof until she is quite unfit for saving, spiritual surgery. By the time she has grown into a middle-aged nun she is like a frightened suspect of cancer who refuses to see the diagnostician for fear of hearing the name of her ailment. How often do we not hear an old religious heartily declare: "Oh, I have my faults, but I am certainly not jealous-curious-proud-etc." Trace it, whatever it is, down the long litany of human ignobilities, and we shall find that this base of "innocence" is the snug stronghold of that religious' predominant fault. Contrariwise, the humble religious is always sure that she is proud. The loving Sister who delights in the joys and successes of others is the first one to admit to the seeds of jealousy and envy inherent in us all. The mortified religious is always trying to guard his senses. And only the very pure fear greatly for their purity.

"Who are You, Lord? And, Lord, who am I?" The Franciscan who is mature in the spiritual life poses those rhetorical questions as a true prayer, based on a self-knowledge which has fitted him for humility. There is nothing so disheartening as trying to direct a soul entrenched in an elected self-ignorance, nothing so futile as attempting to enlighten a religious who finds his bliss in blindness. Actually, it is stupor, not bliss. Something more akin to bliss is reserved for the soul stricken less with its own meanness than with the grandeur of a God great enough to find such meanness lovable.

If the greatest saints thought themselves the greatest sinners, it was not because they were blind nor foolish. They had nearly perfect vision, whereas we often suffer from a mild form of the spiritual astigmatism which afflicted the famous (or infamous)

Up Until this Time We Have Done Nothing

"praying" pharisee in the temple. As does everything else in the spiritual life, this knowledge of ourselves revolves on a pin of paradox. It is only when we recognize ourselves to be utterly unlovable that God can find us a fit object for His Love. It is when we are no longer surprised at anything we find emerging in others, nor hiding in the scented folds of our own self-esteem, that God can surprise us with that kind of joy which sent our Father Francis singing down the Umbrian lanes. We can never be free of the treachery of our own nature unless we feel the weight of its chains. And surely all of us, at scattered and splendid moments, have tasted the mysterious and heady happiness of knowing it is the very chains that endear us to a compassionate God. At such moments, we kiss the chains of our ignominy and learn what St. Thérèse of Lisieux knew so well: that we cannot lay claim to God's saving mercy unless we know ourselves desperately in need of that mercy. "The best way to insure God's mercy," said St. Thérèse, "is to come before Him empty-handed." If we are forever clutching at scraps and patches of self-justification to cover the nakedness of our spirit, always printing counterfeit money of excuses to swell our own exchequer, what is left to God? Yet He will work a miracle of mercy to justify a soul that never justifies itself. God will not fail to find excuses for the religious who has no excuses for himself.

"Up until this time, my brothers," our seraphic Father liked to repeat, "we have done nothing. Now let us begin." This humble, undespairing cry is a spiritual escutcheon for all his sons and daughters. Having failed so often, seeing each day some new baseness in this self we perhaps once thought impeccable, we sink into the depths of our ignobility only to find there the key to our only nobility: our strange, splendid dignity as children of a God who never stoops so quickly to our misery as when the taste of it lies most bitterly recognized on our soul. Indeed, we have done nothing, we poor little creatures so easily unmanned in our most idealistic and resolute hours by the untiring enemy within us. But now let us begin. For, now we have swung the full, pendulumed paradox-arc of sanctity, to find our unlovableness loved by God, our naked and admitted shame covered with His mercy, and our protestations of guilt drowned in the thunder of His forgiveness.

The sturdy old pious books were fond of inviting us to seek contempt and to glory in being despised by others. For the contemplative soul,—which every true son and daughter of St. Francis must be—there is a far more exquisite suffering than the contempt of others: the knowing that we are indeed contemptible, but finding ourselves loved instead. In the moments of our most acute self-knowledge, the contempt of others would be something of a balm on the aching twist of sorrow and remorse in our hearts! Instead, we are encompassed at that precise moment with the unspeakable Love of God. This is the keenest suffering of the contemplative, and also the apex of her joy. There, we begin. And at that point, we shall one day hope to end.

About the Author

Alberta Aschmann was born on St. Valentine's Day, 1921. She was taught by the School Sisters of Notre Dame and became a candidate with the same community after graduating high school. With them she attended Saint Louis University, but shortly before graduating, she left to pursue a deeper call to the cloistered contemplative life with the Colettine Poor Clares in Chicago, Illinois, on July 7, 1942. There she received the religious name Sister Mary Francis of Our Lady. She began writing even as a novice and continued to write through the adventures of being sent to help found the new monastery in Roswell, New Mexico, and later while serving in various roles in the community.

On May 19, 1964, she was elected abbess of the community in Roswell and held that role for more than forty years. She was also elected head of the federation of Colettine Poor Clare monasteries in the United States which had been recently formed. These elections were certainly based on, and also served to increase, her deep insight into the religious life. This insight led to the writing of several books which have been instrumental in the formation of religious, Poor Clares and others, for many years. Among these books are *A Right to be Merry*, bestselling Catholic book of 1956; *Walled in Light*, an enthralling biography of St. Colette; *Chastity, Poverty, and Obedience: Rediscovering the Vision for Renewal of Religious Life*; and many more.

On February 11, 2006, she went to meet her Bridegroom, the Mass of Christian Burial being celebrated for her on her eighty-fifth birthday. May her reflections on the perennial beauty of our Faith and the Poor Clare tradition continue to inspire for years to come.

www.ingramcontent.com/pod-product-compliance
Ingram Content Group UK Ltd.
Pitfield, Milton Keynes, MK11 3LW, UK
UKHW021902100325
4893UKWH00017BA/58